Residency
Interview
Handbook

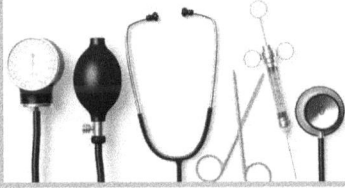

Residency Interview Handbook

Chu Qin Phua

National Healthcare Group, Singapore

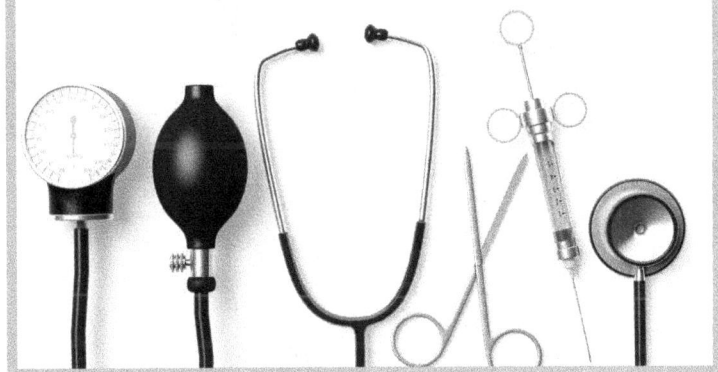

World Scientific

NEW JERSEY · LONDON · SINGAPORE · BEIJING · SHANGHAI · HONG KONG · TAIPEI · CHENNAI · TOKYO

Published by

World Scientific Publishing Co. Pte. Ltd.

5 Toh Tuck Link, Singapore 596224

USA office: 27 Warren Street, Suite 401-402, Hackensack, NJ 07601

UK office: 57 Shelton Street, Covent Garden, London WC2H 9HE

Library of Congress Cataloging-in-Publication Data

Names: Phua, Chu Qin, author.

Title: Residency interview handbook / Chu Qin Phua.

Description: New Jersey : World Scientific, 2019. | Includes index.

Identifiers: LCCN 2015038340 | ISBN 9789814723411 (hardcover : alk. paper) |
    ISBN 981472341X (hardcover : alk. paper) | ISBN 9789814723428 (pbk. : alk. paper) |
    ISBN 9814723428 (pbk. : alk. paper)

Subjects: | MESH: Internship and Residency--Singapore. | Interviews as Topic--Singapore. |
    Vocational Guidance--Singapore.

Classification: LCC R840 | NLM W 20 | DDC 610.71/55--dc23

LC record available at http://lccn.loc.gov/2015038340

British Library Cataloguing-in-Publication Data

A catalogue record for this book is available from the British Library.

For any available supplementary material, please visit
https://www.worldscientific.com/worldscibooks/10.1142/9797#t=suppl

Preface

"Evolving is life's greatest accomplishment and its greatest reward."

Ray Dalio

With the inception of the Residency Programme in 2010, a new training structure with dedicated resources, designated faculty and defined curriculum and assessments has been introduced. This Residency programme comes with a different set of application process, selection criteria and interview format. This book is written with the intention of helping medical students and junior doctors **construct and consolidate their preparation for Residency application**.

What Is This Book About?

This book serves as a guide to the various components of Residency application. It aims to provide insight and guidance to Residency application, how to choose a specialty, CV preparation, as well as how to build the groundwork for Residency entry — including research, presentation and interview skills.

So, this book is for you if you are:

A medical student or junior doctor or international medical graduate

— Seeking to understand the current Residency Training structure and entry requirements in Singapore

- Seeking directions on how to choose which specialties to enter
- Gearing up to give yourself an edge on entering Residency Training

Why It is Important?

Junior doctor years can be gruesome and exhausting. More often than not, it is easy to feel that you are thrown in at the deep end with little support — whether it is making your 8th attempt to draw blood from the patient who just does not appear to have any veins, or feeling out of depth in managing a sick patient in the middle of a night call, or dealing with distressed patients and families.

Worst of all, I find, is the pervasive uncertainty in our career path. Uncertainty is ubiquitous in medicine — from not knowing where your next MOPEX medical officer posting would be, not knowing which specialty career path would suit you, uncertain of whether you will fit into the department culture, or feeling uncertain of what is required of you for entry into specialty training. Whilst this book cannot remove all uncertainties, I hope it would provide some help in your career navigation and alleviate some anxieties by equipping you with as much information and strategies possible to mitigate the uncertainties to come.

The early part of my medical officer career was spent exploring the options. I went through a variety of rotations, including acute medicine, urology, ENT, ICU, general surgery, respiratory medicine and orthopaedics, before choosing ENT as my career. I deferred career decision-making until the end of the second medical officer year, whilst taking the time to experience the specialties and gather information about different career paths. To me, it is time well spent, and certainly not something I regret. I would have struggled otherwise to be at peace with my final decision without having seen what the different specialties have to offer.

However, to caution, MOPEX training, whilst useful when at the early years for the breadth of experience and training, does not count as accrued experience towards eventual specialist qualifications. Every year of deferment from career decision-making can potentially make the subsequent application to training more difficult.

With all these unknown and difficulties, I hope to provide you with some ideas and a framework of how to steer your career in a more purposeful and directed manner. Most of what I have written in the book, are things I have learnt on my own journey, and some are perhaps advice I wished I had when I was at the early stages of my medical career. Having some idea of how the system works and what can be done to increase your chances of entry into the system, hopefully makes it easier for you on this path of uncertainty. My fervent wish is that this framework can be of some use for you to do some introspection, obtain sufficient information and overview of different career options to help make a robust career decision — one you will find fulfilling and fruitful inthe years to come.

Why I Wrote This Book

It is simply that I noticed a niche and that I was driven by the desire to create something of utility. I really wanted to go through the process of producing something from scratch — something of relevance and impact, in this subject matter which is close to my heart. In addition, there is something that is just really alluring about the creation process — from the conception of the idea to execution in detail and finally fruition. It is exhilarating, satisfying and just sexy. To be honest, I am not even convinced that it is the end-point that I care about. It was solely to experience, to learn and to grow in the process.

Nonetheless, this was not an easy process. I started writing this book at year-1 of my Residency, but never quite had the courage to get it out into the real world even when there were publishers keen to publish it. This was a journey of self-doubt and anguish. There were times when I almost gave up. What if people didn't find this book useful? What if I am not good enough to write such a book?

What if I was just wasting my time? Things would get so bad that sometimes I would be too paralysed with fear to be able to carry on. It was incredibly difficult to find the courage to carry on when there is no validation that you are on the right track.

Yet, again and again, I would also ask myself — 'Why not?' and I just could not find the answer. No one had written a book like that of relevance to the local context. This was my chance to do something of use — to empower people in this process of career navigation and working towards their dream jobs/calling.

In addition, midway through writing, crippled by fear and petrified by the thought that what I am about to produce might be rubbish, I came across Joi Ito's TED talk. Joi Ito is an MIT Media Lab director, member of the 'Safecast' group and creator of the world largest <u>online radiation map</u> with more than 16 million data points. ('Safecast' is a voluntary non-profit organisation that created a dataset on radiation levels for the benefit of the public, following the Japan earthquake and explosion of nuclear power plant in 2011.) It was a talk about the evolving ways of innovation and pushing innovation beyond the limits. One of the things he said struck chord — **"You have to get it into the real world to have it actually count." "Deploy or die."** His advice for new ideas/entrepreneurial efforts was to <u>get it out into the real world</u>, innovate and advance along the way.

This gave me the courage to present to you my less than perfect book. So, here I am — learning as I do, seeking out opportunities, in hope to experience, learn and innovate. And here's hoping that you would join me along the way!

Some Declaration

1) It is a learnt process — I see, I experience, I learn, I consolidate and then now I share. There is no ingenuity in this. I did not just automatically know what was required for the interviews or residency entry. All these were gained and learnt from years of

recurrent preparations for interviews and purposeful exploration of career paths. This book is a collation of these experiences. So rest assured that a lot of these are learnt behaviour and it's never too late to start.

2) I do not proclaim to be the best person to write this book or to dish out advice on how to be successful in Residency application. Believe me when I say I do feel slightly precocious to be writing a book at all. However, I do think of this as more of sharing of the experiences and hacks that I collected and collated through the years.

Finally, my sincere apologies, if I get too philosophical/blunt/colloquial at any point. This is after all my first experience with writing. Therefore, should I have inadvertently caused any offense or discomfort, apologies and rest assured that it is unintentional. My wish for you is to be able to create a connection between your daily work, passion and talent, in doing so, creating meaningful work, meaningful relationships and a meaningful life ahead.

Acknowledgements

For the courage to create this book, I thank Mr. Yakubu Karagama, mentor and coach, whose faith in me gave me the assurance that I have it in me to make things possible. I will forever be grateful to him for taking me under his wing as a fresh and inexperienced medical officer at ENT Surgery, Tameside Hospital. I am grateful to his blend of high expectations and patient guidance, which catapulted massive growth and confidence in me. I will always remember that posting as the one that set off a decisive change in me, which I continue to benefit from today.

For being kind, encouraging and generous, I thank my mentor, Dr. Toh Song Tar, whose work ethics and philosophy I can only hope to emulate and live up to one day. Thank you for the opportunity to learn by your side as you push frontiers and create initiatives to advance the field of Sleep Medicine and Surgery. Thank you for being the inspiration that pushes me to strive harder.

For sharing my journey of growth from a medical student to a specialist, I am grateful to my friend Yuet Peng, who has always been there to keep me company. Thank you for being my sounding board in the process of my career exploration and thank you for the support through these years of uncertainties. Thank you for always being there to help put things into perspective for me.

For sharing their wisdom and experiences, I thank my teachers — Dr. Paul Mok, Prof. Henry Tan, Ming Yann, Terry, Prof. Bala, Dr. Duncan Wong, Mr. Yeo Seng Beng, Prof. Siow, Ian,

Tee Sin, Dr. Sandeep, Dr. Constance, Dr. Sarah Lu, Chun Hai, Dr. David Loke, Dr. Julian Lee, Dr. Timothy Shim and Dr. Cheong Ee Cherk. Thank you for helping me grow and develop as a doctor, which has helped me consolidate my experience, which formed the foundation for this book.

For brainstorming with me and for the perceptive feedbacks and insights on this book, I thank my friends — Bang, UE, MJ, Wai Yen, Kimberley, Van, Ed, Lilleen, Tze Choong, Ching Yee, Ernest and Sabrina. Thank you for challenging me to think deeply and for holding me accountable in finishing what I have started.

For encouragement and discerning advice on the framework of the book, I thank Dr. Derrick Aw, who has generously shared his experience in book publishing and provided me with ideas on how to move things forward.

For being patient with me, I thank my editor Sook Cheng. Thank you for being understanding in allowing me to work at a pace that I am comfortable with. This has given me the opportunity to mull and contemplate over the composition and details of the book, which I believe helped in creation of a better final product. I cannot express enough gratitude for your guidance in helping me navigate the process of publishing this book.

About the Author

"Some men see things as they are and say, why; I dream things that never were and say, why not."

George Bernard Shaw

Chu Qin is a first-time author whose dreams are to create something of a utility. She is a surgeon, teacher and health advocate. Her bigger hopes are to engineer circumstances and opportunities to help people fulfil their potential.

This is a book she began writing since year-1 of her Otolaryngology Residency training, and has finally come to fruition now that she has graduated. This prolonged process is in part due to the multiple revisions, frequent internal debates on the plausibility of this book, and in part due to multiple other distractions along the way.

She loves her job as an ENT Surgeon and finds joy in helping patients achieve better Sleep health. However, part of her always wondered if she could do more. This explains why she is often rather distracted and loves working on multiple ideas at a go. The world of possibilities excites her and the joy of synergistic collaboration keeps her going. These multiple ventures serve as a creative outlet for her and has led to amazing learning experiences and fulfilling journeys.

As per Jim Collins, famous author of *Good to Great*, Chu Qin hopes that someday she would achieve an exceptional sense of tranquility, knowing that she has 'had a hand in creating something of intrinsic excellence that makes a contribution'.

Contents

1

About Residency

*"The only constant in life is **change**." — Heraclitus*

Key Points

- Prior to year 2010, the formal postgraduate medical training system consisted of the BST/AST system
- The BST/AST system allows rotations in hospitals across Singapore, providing broader exposure and experience for trainees. However, it was criticised for its lack of structure and accountability.
- The Residency training programme replaces the BST/AST system in 2010. It features institutional infrastructures and resources for training, defined curricula, designated faculty and protected teaching time.
- The 3 main sponsoring instituations for Residency are the National Healthcare Group — Alexandra Hospital Pte Ltd (NHG-AHPL), Singapore Health Service (SHS) and National University Health System (NUHS)
- Training duration under Residency Programme ranges from 5 to 6 years.
- Entry requirement between specialties vary — some offer direct entry from medical school whilst some require completion of PGY1 (house officer year).

The Change — BST/AST to Residency

Change is inevitable, it is after all how we progress. Hence, this chapter is not intended to contest or critique either training system. Rather, it serves to provide an understanding of both systems to enable navigation into the current system. It is important to note that all information in this chapter is referenced from official sources and is true at the time of writing. However, for the latest updates and details of each specialties, it is best to refer to the official Ministry of Health Holdings (MOHH) Residency or the relevant specialty official websites.

Prior to year 2010, the Singapore postgraduate medical education was modeled after the UK system of Basic and Advanced Specialty Training. Formal local training started in 1970s with the introduction of the local Master of Medicine (MMed) degrees conferred by the National University of Singapore. As such, the National University of Singapore helm the Basic Specialty Training (BST) and the administration of the MMed, whereas the Academy of Medicine assumed the responsibility in the regulation and implementation of Advanced Specialty Training (AST). There was also the option of the Health Manpower Development Programme (HMDP) for doctors to go abroad fully funded in their AST years to import knowledge and advanced skill sets to meet the emerging national needs.

Catalysts for change came in years 2006–2007, when a trainee survey raised concerns on lack of organised training, and inadequate time and supervision for training owing to conflicts with service demands.[1] In addition, there was increased demand for specialist manpower, precipitated by an expanding and aging population. This led to an urgency to produce more numbers of specialists without compromising the quality of the training.

The Residency Programme was introduced in 2010 to replace the BST/AST system. This was a decision made by the Ministry of Health (MOH) and the Specialists Accreditation Board (SAB) after research into graduate medical education across various countries including Australia, the US, the UK, and in Europe. It was concluded that the US Residency Training model was one that was most efficient and high yield in producing specialists while providing highly organised and standardised training and assessment throughout the process.

This chapter aims to give you a brief view of the old BST/AST system, while focusing on providing you with the relevant, essential information regarding the new Residency Programme to shed some light on some common concerns surrounding the new system.

The Past

BST/AST

Prior to the Residency Training Programme, the formal post-graduate medical training system consisted of the UK-style BST/AST system.[2] This training system includes two parts:

1) Basic Specialty Training (BST)

   • Administered by the National University of Singapore (NUS)

2) Advanced Specialty Training (AST)

   • Administered by the Joint Committee on Specialist Training (JCST)

The JCST Secretariat is served jointly by the Academy of Medicine and the Division of Graduate Medical Studies of the National University Singapore. Under the JCST umbrella are all the Specialist Training Committees (STCs) for 35 registered specialties who are responsible for administering the specialist exit examinations.[2,3]

In general, BST consists of two to three years of training. During this period, trainees are required to rotate through the relevant clinical postings as well as pass the post-graduate examination (local Master of Medicine) before progressing into AST. Under the BST training system, trainees have the opportunity to rotate to all hospitals in Singapore for their clinical postings.

At the end of BST, trainees apply for entry into AST. For doctors who did not train under the BST system, but have undergone equivalent, recognised clinical training programmes from overseas, there was an option of midpoint entry into AST within some specialties, subjected to review by the Academy of Medicine and Specialty Training Committee.

Trainees subsequently undergo three to four years of training in the AST. After the exit examination, there was an option of participating in the Health Manpower Development

Programme (HMDP) for further sub-specialty training abroad with full funding.

There were also seamless programmes where trainees progressed naturally into AST without having to re-apply. However, similar to the BST/AST system, trainees are required to pass an intermediate postgraduate examination (in most specialties) to enable progression into the next stage of training.

In the BST/AST system, the general progression to become a specialist is as below:

1. Graduate from medical school
2. Internship/housemanship 1 year +/– rotations as medical officers
3. BST 2–3 years
4. Intermediate examination — Master of Medicine (MMed)
5. AST 3–4 years
6. Exit examination
7. Apply to Specialist Accreditation Board (SAB) for accreditation and to the Singapore Medical Council (SMC) for specialist registration
8. Option of participating in the Health Manpower Development Programme (HMDP) to go abroad for training for up to 2 years with full funding.[2]

The BST/AST training was based more on apprenticeship and summative assessments. This relies on the willingness of the educator to teach, the initiative and discipline of the trainee to learn, as well as the rapport of between the educator and the trainee. There is more self-directed learning which can empower trainees to personalise their training based on their learning needs. The promotion of this reflective learning, intentional or not, allows the cultivation of the habit of lifelong learning to maintain competency in medicine.

One of the strengths of the BST/AST system is that it allows trainees to rotate to most if not all hospitals across Singapore in their training (as opposed to Residency, where trainees are limited to two to three hospitals within their Sponsoring Institution). This provides broader exposure and experience, which trainees can then assimilate into their practice. In addition, trainees have more job options at the end of their training, owing to their exposure to various departments in hospitals across Singapore.

Criticism of the BST/AST model includes its lack of training structure, lack of accountability, insufficient supervision and protected time for learning. Training time was often not honoured due to service demands and teaching was often adhoc. Hence, there can be disparity in the training quality between trainees.

As of September 2018, some of the training including Paediatric Surgery, Dermatology, Pathology, Radiation Oncology, Aviation Medicine, Intensive Care Medicine, Neonatology, Palliative Medicine and Sports Medicine still implement the BST/AST training.[7] Some of these programmes still accept mid-stream entry. However, this will be considered on a case-by-case basis, taking into account the applicant's prior training experience. Programme information, entry qualifications and application information are available from the Joint Committee of Specialist Training.

Family Medicine

Prior to the Residency program, there are two main routes of entry into Family Medicine, as stipulated by Family Physicians Accreditation Board (FPAB). This includes the degree/diploma route and the practice route. The practice route is no longer accepted as of 1 July 2014.[8] Some of these entry routes still exist, in addition to the current Residency Training program. Details are as below:

a) **Degree/Diploma Route**

1) **Graduate Diploma in Family Medicine (GDFM)**

- Structured training programme administered by the College of Family Physicians Singapore (CFPS) and the Division of Graduate Medical Studies (DGMS)
- Duration: 2 years

- Consists of 8 modules, each module conducted over 3 months
- Registration opens April each year, course commences in June
- Consists of combination of self study, online case studies and some interactive and tutorial sessions
- Information available from: http://www.cfps.org.sg/programmes/graduate-diploma-in-fm/
  http://medicine.nus.edu.sg/dgms/family-medicine.html

2) **Master of Medicine (MMed) in Family Medicine**

- Duration: 16 months
- Prerequisite
  o Doctors with at least 6 years of work experience after graduation, of which at least one year must be in a Family Medicine setting.
  o Completion of 8 modules of Family Medicine Modular Course not more than 5 years prior to application.
- Consists of group teachings, skills courses, self-directed learning, written work, preceptorship sessions and practice audit, followed by examination.
- Information available from:
  http://www.cfps.org.sg/programmes/master-of medicine-in-fm/

3) **Other equivalent Family Medicine degrees/diplomas**

- Requires minimum 3 years of Family Medicine practice experience
- Recognised qualifications include[9]:
  o Member of the College of General Practitioners, Singapore (MCGP)
  o Member of Royal College of General Practitioners, United Kingdom (MRCGP, UK)
  o Diplomate, American Board of Family Medicine (DABFM, USA)
  o Fellow of Royal Australian College of General Practitioners, Australia (FRACGP, Aust.)

- o Fellow of Royal New Zealand College of General Practitioners, New Zealand (FRN ZCGP)
- o Fellow of Hong Kong College of General Practitioners, Hong Kong (FHKCGP)

Upon obtaining the degree or diploma, applicants can apply for accreditation with the Family Physicians Accreditation Board. Applicants who receive accreditation can then apply to the Register of Family Physicians with Singapore Medical Council.

b) Practice Route

- In practice within Family Medicine for 5 or more years AND
- Completion of 2–4 Accredited Modular Courses (AMC)
- This entry route was closed on 31 Dec 2013

Up to date information regarding the Family Medicine entry route can be obtained from

1) Family Physicians Accreditation Board:
   http://www.healthprofessionals.gov.sg/fpab
2) College of Family Physicians Singapore:
   http://www.cfps.org.sg/

The Present

Roadmap to Residency

The Residency Training Programme was implemented by the Ministry of Health (MOH) in July 2010 to provide structured training. It is a nationally standardised, structured post-graduate training programme with the aim of enhancing specialist training via creation of a conducive training environment. The Residency Training Programme helps bring forth trained specialists and family physicians to meet surging healthcare needs. It is executed via

- Structured institutional organisation (Sponsoring institutions) with priority for training and education
- Defined curricula and regular formative assessment

- Designated faculty with protected teaching time to provide supervision

Under the Residency system, residents are matched to a training programme under a sponsoring institution: SingHealth, National University Hospital and the National Healthcare Group. Each sponsoring institution has its own clusters of hospitals (as below) through which the residents will rotate.[11]

Sponsoring Institutions	Hospitals
National Healthcare Group — Alexandra Hospital Pte Ltd (NHG-AHPL)	Tan Tock Seng Hospital Khoo Teck Puat Hospital Institute of Mental Health
Singapore Health Service (SHS)	KK Women's and Children's Hospital Changi General Hospital Singapore General Hospital
National University Health System (NUHS)	National University Hospital Jurong General Hospital

BST/AST versus Residency

Table 1.1 comparing the main characteristics of the old BST/AST system to the new Residency training system.

Table 1.1 Comparison between Old BST/AST System and New Residency System

	BST/AST	Residency
Origins	UK based	US based
Year implemented	1970	2010
Examinations	Master of Medicine (MMed) Exit Exam	American Board Exam Master of Medicine (MMed) Exit Exam
Duration of training	2–3 years BST 3–4 years AST	3–6 years of training

(Continued)

Table 1.1   *(Continued)*

	BST/AST	Residency
Location of training	Island-wide (broader exposure)	Institution-based (focused training with more continuity)
Committees responsible	Joint Committee on Specialist Training (JCST)	Residency Advisory Committee (RAC)
Ownership	Academy of Medicine, National University Singapore	Sponsoring Institutions
Training structure	• More opportunistic learning • Structured curricula not usually present • Competency milestones not defined	• Defined curricula with defined competencies to be achieved • Regular formative assessments • Designated supervisors • Protected training time
Others	• Allows midpoint entry into AST	• Only certain specialties have midpoint entry • Has clinician scientist track

Programme Types + Duration

Below (Table 1.2) is a list of programme types and duration offered under the Residency Training Programme. It is broadly divided into five categories[10]:

- Programmes without Transitional Year (TY) or PGY1 (Equivalent to House Officer Year)
- Programmes which require completion of TY or PGY1 prior to commencing Residency
- Programmes which require completion of TY or PGY1 prior to application
- Senior Residency for Advanced Internal Medicine (requires completion of 3 years of basic Internal Medicine training)

Information above taken from

- Specialist Accreditation Board:
  http://www.healthprofessionals.gov.sg/sab/specialist-training/residency-training-programmes

Table 1.2   Programme Types and Duration

Programmes without TY or PGY1 (Direct Entry)	
Programme	**Training Duration (Years)**
• Internal Medicine	• 5
• Emergency Medicine	• 5
• General Surgery	• 5
• Preventive Medicine	• 5
• Psychiatry	• 5
• Paediatric Medicine	• 6
Programmes which require completion of TY or PGY1 prior to commencing Residency	
Programme	**Training Duration (Years)**
• Family Medicine	• TY/PGY1 + 3
• Anaesthesiology	• TY/PGY1 + 5
• Diagnostic Radiology	• TY/PGY1 + 5
• Pathology	• TY/PGY1 + 5
• Ophthalmology	• TY/PGY1 + 5
• Otorhinolaryngology	• TY/PGY1 + 5
• Obstetrics & Gynaecology	• TY/PGY1 + 6
• Orthopaedic Surgery	• TY/PGY1 + 6
Programmes which require completion of TY or PGY1 prior to application	
Programme	**Training Duration (Years)**
• Cardiothoracic Surgery	• 6
• Hand Surgery	• 6
• Neurosurgery	• 6
• Plastic Surgery	• 6
• Urology	• 6
Senior Residency for Advanced Internal Medicine	
Programme	**Training Duration (Years)**
• Advanced Internal Medicine	• 2
• Nuclear Medicine	• 2.5
• Endocrinology	• 3
• Gastroenterology	• 3
• Geriatric Medicine	• 3
• Haematology	• 3
• Infectious Disease	• 3

(Continued)

Table 1.2   (*Continued*)

Programme	Training Duration (Years)
• Medical Oncology	• 3
• Neurology	• 3
• Rehabilitation Medicine	• 3
• Renal Medicine	• 3
• Respiratory Medicine	• 3
• Rheumatology	• 3
• Cardiology	• 3.5
• Dermatology	• 3.5

http://www.healthprofessionals.gov.sg/sab/specialist-training/residency-training-programmes

Clinician Scientist Track

The incorporation of Clinician Scientist track into Residency Training serves to provide interested trainees with the opportunities and infrastructure to pursue a career as a clinician-scientist. In addition to the usual Residency Programme, trainees on the Clinician-Scientist track are allocated an additional year to perform research under guidance. Trainees on the clinical-scientist track also receive research training and will achieve additional research qualifications.

For successful exit from the Clinical Scientist Residency Programme, candidates are required to obtain a Masters of Clinical Investigations or equivalent, and at least a first-author publication, in addition to fulfilling the usual clinical standards applied to their Clinical Track counterparts. Up-to-date information can be obtained from individual sponsoring institution Residency websites.

As of 2015, there is no option to apply direct into the Clinician-Scientist track from a non trainee position. Those interested will need to first apply to a Residency Programme and then apply into the Clinician-Scientist track in the 4th year of Residency Programme. For existing residents within the Clinical Track, there are options to apply into the Clinician Scientist track subjected to approval from the Programme Director and Designated Institution Official (DIO).

Up-to-date information regarding the Clinician-Scientist track is available from: http://www.healthprofessionals.gov.sg/sab/specialist-training/residency-training-programmes/clinician-scientist-training

Training Structure

Training structure under the Residency Programme may have minor variations between each sponsoring institution, but they invariably follow a common theme:

- **Structured curriculum** — Resident's rotations for the entire training duration are well defined. Most involve some core rotations with some elective postings.
- **Defined milestones** — Residents have defined and graduated learning objectives and responsibilities.
- **Regular assessments** — There will be regular in-rotation assessment of Resident's clinical skills throughout the Residency training, as well as other major examinations such as the American Board Examination, MMed (specific to Singapore), as well as the Exit Examination.
- **Teaching resources** — Teaching resources are allocated to support Resident's training.

Progression to become Specialist

Structured curriculum

Each specialty will have its own structured curriculum. However, the exact execution of their rotations might vary slightly between each of the three sponsoring institutions.

To illustrate, Table 1.3 shows a sample Otorhinolaryngology rotation adapted with reference from the 3 sponsoring institutions.

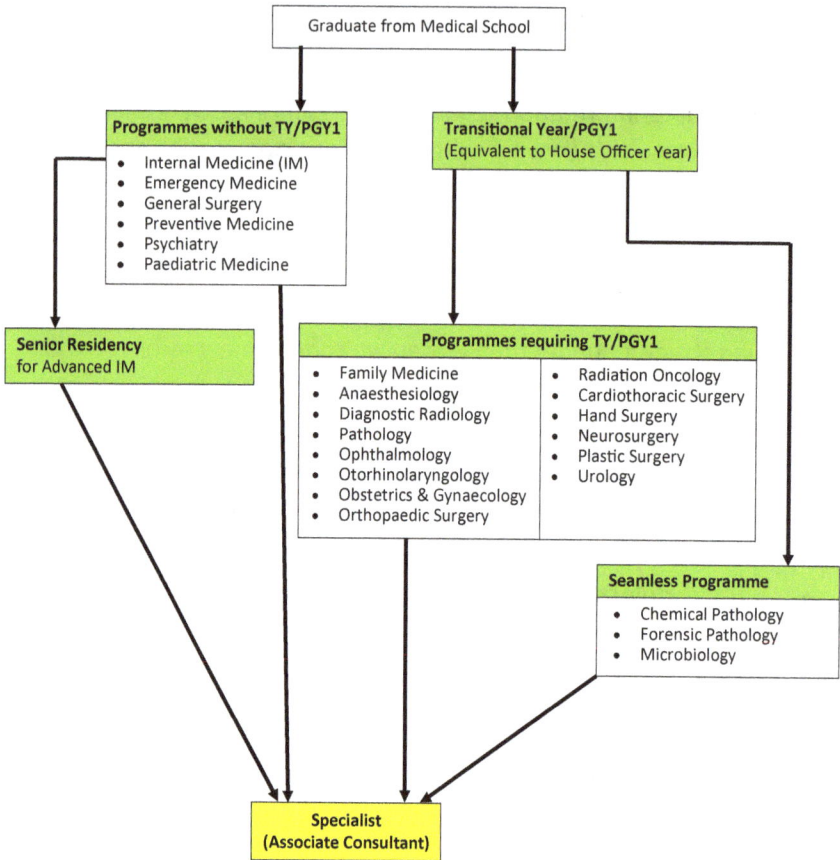

Figure 1.1   Flow chart of progression to become a Specialist (adapted from information from the Specialist Accreditation Board website).[10]

There will be minute variations between each programme. Nonetheless, the general principles are that, the initial training years are geared towards building a basic foundation and subsequent years are focused on various subspecialty-specific rotation blocks.

Up-to-date and detailed information regarding the curriculum/rotations of each specialty or Residency programme

Table 1.3   Sample Otorhinolaryngology Residency Rotations

Residency Year	Rotation blocks					
1	General Otorhinolaryngology			General Surgery		
2	Otology	Rhinology	Head and Neck	Laryngology	Sleep Disorders	Facial Plastics
3	Paediatric Otorhinolaryngology			Plastics Surgery	Research	Sleep Disorders
4	Rhinology	Head and Neck	Facial Plastics	Otology	Sleep Disorders	Laryngology
5	Non-ACGME-I accredited electives, or continue with subspecialty rotations					

Adapted with reference from various sponsoring institution programmes.

are available at the respective Sponsoring Institution Residency websites:

- NUHS: http://www.nuhs.edu.sg/nuhsresidency/
- Singhealth: http://www.singhealthresidency.com.sg/
- NHG-AHPL: https://www.nhgeducation.nhg.com.sg/nhgresidency

Defined milestones

There is a systematic progression of required clinical competency from each year of Residency to the next. There are various components to the milestones — which can include clinical knowledge, patient care, communication skills, professionalism, procedural and surgical skills. This will be commensurate with the advancement of Resident's responsibilities and independence.

Just to illustrate with Otorhinolaryngology, below is a sample of defined surgical skills that residents might be expected to achieve each year. It usually progresses in a graduated manner from simple procedures to more difficult surgeries in the later years of training.

Residency Year	Procedures/Surgical Skills
R1	Flexible Nasoendoscopy Postnasal space biopsy Fine needle aspiration Drain, suture, staple removal Wound dressing and packing Examination of ears and aural toilet under microscope Nasal packing Drainage of peritonsillar abscess Removal of foreign body Simple laceration repair Tracheostomy tube change Excision of skin lesions
R2	Adenotonsillectomy Rigid oesophagoscopy Cervical lymph node excision Manipulation and reduction of nasal bone fracture Rigid nasal endoscopy Septoplasty Turbinate surgery
R3	Direct laryngoscope Endoscopy laryngeal microsurgery Tracheostomy Incision and drainage of deep neck abscess Submandibular gland excision Myringotomy
R4	Excision of thyroglossal duct cyst Thyroidectomy Parotidectomy Functional Endoscopic Sinus Surgery Tympanoplasty Mastoidectomy Neck dissection Septorhinoplasty Repair of facial fracture Uvulopalatopharyngoplasty

The defined milestones differ between specialties. At present, this resource is not made available publicly. To gain a better understanding, your best bet might be to speak to the Training Programme Director, faculty members or existing residents.

Assessment tools

Under the Residency Programme, there are regular evaluations to ensure residents achieve the required competency before progressing to the next level. Assessments are generally designed to test six core competencies:

1) Medical knowledge
2) Patient care
3) Professionalism
4) Interpersonal skills and communication
5) Practice-based learning
6) Systems-based practice

Evaluation can be divided into formative and summative assessments. Formative assessment methods include (but are not limited to):

1) Mini clinical evaluation exercise (Mini-CEX)

This is a 10–20 minute assessment where the assessor observes the resident when the resident takes a history and examines a patient. Residents are assessed on their medical interviewing skills, physical examination, professionalism, clinical judgement, communication skills, organisation skills and overall clinical competence.

2) Case-based discussions (CBD)

This is a 15–20 minute exercise where residents present a case to their assessor and discussion and comprehensive review ensues around the actual case. Often it is a discussion of how a clinical case is managed by the resident and his or her rationale behind management decisions. Com- ponents assessed include clinical assessment and interpretation, management plan and follow-up planning, decision-making, overall judgement and clinical care.

3) Direct observation procedures (DOPs)

This involves the assessor observing the resident carrying out a procedure with subsequent evaluation of understanding of issues surrounding the procedure itself (e.g. central line insertion). Components assessed can include understanding of indications, anatomy, procedure and potential complications, ability to obtain consent, performing safe procedure, performing technical aspects in keeping with current standards, ability to deal with unexpected events, documentation, communication with patient and staff and professionalism throughout procedure.

4) Surgical skills evaluation

This is similar to direct observation procedures (as above) except that it involves evaluation of surgical skills.

All of these formative assessments require direct verbal feedback from the assessor to highlight to the resident areas of strengths and suggestions for development. The number of evaluations required for each rotation is determined by Training Programme Directors and can vary between programmes.

Summative assessment methods include:

1) In-training examination/American Board Examination

Administered as a yearly event, this is an examination that assesses the resident's knowledge in all areas of the specialty. Examination results allow the resident to identify areas of deficiency and strength, as well as to compare their performances with their peers from all over the world. It is usually administered in multiple-choice question format. Some of the examinations do have extended matching questions.

Not all specialties subscribe to this American Board Examination. Below is a list of specialties in Singapore that have subscribed to the American Board Examination.

Specialties with In-Training Examination.[6]	
Anaesthesiology	Obstetrics & Gynaecology
Cardiology	Ophthalmology
Diagnostic Radiology	Orthopaedic Surgery
Emergency Medicine	Otorhinolargyngology (ENT)
Endocrinology	Paediatric Medicine
Family Medicine	Pathology
Gastroenterology	Psychiatry
General Surgery	Rheumatology
Haematology	Respiratory Medicine
Infectious Diseases	Renal Medicine
Internal Medicine	Nuclear Medicine
Medical Oncology	

Specialties with In-Training Examination.[6]

2) Intermediate examinations

There are some examinations which are required for progression into Senior Residency. While the In-training Examination (as above) is an emulation of the US Residency system, most of these intermediate examinations (as below) are a preservation of Singapore's previous training system, making it unique to Singapore's Residency Programme. The examinations and requirements for each respective specialty are detailed as below.

Specialty	Intermediate Assessment
Anaesthesiology	Pass final Master of Medicine (MMed) in Anaesthesiology
Cardiothoracic Surgery	Pass Membership of the Royal College of Surgeons (MRCS) Examination Successful completion of Surgery-In-General programme Satisfactory SESATS and Progress Reports
Diagnostic Radiology	Pass FRCR 2A

(Continued)

(*Continued*)

Specialty	Intermediate Assessment
Emergency Medicine	Pass Membership of College of Emergency Medicine (MCEM) and/or MMed (Emergency Medicine)
Family Medicine	Not applicable
General Surgery	Pass the MMed (Primary) / MRCS Achieve at least a minimum rating of 5 (Competent) on Competency Assessment
Hand Surgery	Pass MRCS Successful completion of Surgery-In-General programme
Intensive Care Medicine	Not applicable
Internal Medicine (IM) related specialties Nuclear Medicine	For 2010-2012 in-flight residents: Pass Membership of Royal College of Physicians (MRCP) or MMed (Internal Medicine) and/or American Board of Internal Medicine (ABIM'S) Programme Director (PD) certification of successful completion of R3 For 2013 intake of new IM residents: Pass local clinical exam and/or "ABIM(S)" exam PD certification of successful completion of R3
Neonatology	Not applicable
Neurosurgery	Pass MRCS Successful completion of Surgery-In-General programme
Obstetrics & Gynaecology	Pass MMed (O&G) or Membership of Royal College of Obstetrics and Gynaecology (MRCOG) Examination
Ophthalmology	Pass MMed (Ophthalmology)
Orthopaedic Surgery	Pass MMed (Orthopaedic Surgery) Part 2
Otorhinolaryngology	Pass MRCS
Pathology (Chemical Pathology, Forensic Pathology, Microbiology)	Fellow of the Royal College of Pathologists of Australasia (FRCPA Part 1) or Membership of Royal College of Pathologists (MRCPath Part 1) Examination or its equivalent
Pathology (Histopathology)	Pass American Board of Medical Specialties (ABMS) MCQ (Pass FRCPA / FRCPath Part 1 for first batch of residents entering R4 in 2013)

(*Continued*)

(Continued)

Specialty	Intermediate Assessment
Paediatric Medicine	Pass MMed (Paediatric Medicine) and/or American Board of Paediatrics (ABP(S))
Paediatric Surgery	Not applicable
Palliative Medicine	Not applicable
Plastic Surgery	Pass MRCS and MMed (Surgery) Successful completion of Surgery-In-General programme
Preventive Medicine	Completed and passed the Masters Degree of Public Health (MPH) or equivalent
Psychiatry	Pass MMed (Psychiatry) or Membership of Royal College of Psychiatrist (MRCPsych (parts 1-4))
Radiation Oncology	FRCR / Fellowship of the Royal Australasian and New Zealand College of Radiologist (FRANZCR) Part 1
Sports Medicine	Not applicable
Urology	Pass MRCS Successful completion of Surgery-In-General programme

Intermediate Assessment for Progression into Senior Residency
(Adapted from Ministry of Health Singapore, Specialist Accreditation Board publication on 'Graduate Medical Education in Singapore)[1]

3) Exit examination

These are the examinations which residents have to pass before being certified as competent to exit as Specialists. Exit examinations vary between specialties. Details are as below.

Specialty	Current Exit Examinations/Assessments
Anaesthesiology	Clinical and case management review Paper critique Logbook review
Cardiology	Multiple Choice Questions (MCQs) Data interpretation

(Continued)

(Continued)

Specialty	Current Exit Examinations/Assessments
Cardiothoracic Surgery	FRCS Clinical assessment Oral assessment
Dermatology	Dermatopathology Slide Assessment Paper critique Oral assessment
Diagnostic Radiology	Exit interview Publication of first authorship paper To achieve at least 75% of the Continuing Medical Education (CME) lectures
Emergency Medicine	Paper critique SAQs (short-answer questions) Oral assessment
Endocrinology	Written assessment: case write-ups Oral assessment
Family Medicine	Written assessment Clinical assessment Oral assessment
Gastroenterology	MCQs
General Surgery	Conjoint exam (FRCS Ed) — Written assessment — Clinical assessment — Oral assessment
Geriatric Medicine	Clinical case assessment Oral assessment
Haematology	Written assessment: essay and SAQs Oral assessment
Hand Surgery	MCQs Clinical assessment Oral assessment
Infectious Diseases	Clinical assessment Clinical case discussions
Intensive Care Medicine	MCQs Clinical assessment
Internal Medicine	Paper critique Oral assessment
Medical Oncology	MCQs Oral assessment

(Continued)

(*Continued*)

Specialty	Current Exit Examinations/Assessments
Neonatology	Write-up on neonatal article Oral assessment
Neurology	Oral assessment
Neurosurgery	FRCS(Surgical Neurology)(Ed)
Nuclear Medicine	MCQs Clinical case discussions Oral assessment
Obstetrics & Gynaecology	OSCE stations Panel interview
Ophthalmology	Oral assessment
Orthopaedic Surgery	Conjoint exam (FRCS (Orth)) Written assessment Clinical assessment Oral assessment
Otorhinolaryngology	Oral assessment
Pathology (Chemical Pathology, Forensic Pathology, Microbiology)	Royal College of Pathologist of Australasia (RCPA) Part 1&2 or FRCPath Part 1 & 2
Pathology (Histopathology)	RCPA Part 1 & 2 or FRCPath Part 1 & 2
Paediatric Medicine;	Paper critique Oral assessment
Paediatric Surgery	Clinical assessment: clinical short cases Oral assessment
Palliative Medicine	Clinical case assessment and discussion Oral assessment
Plastic Surgery	MCQs Objective Structured Clinical Examination (OSCE) stations Oral assessment
Preventive Medicine	Discussion of projects / assignments undertaken during training Paper Critique Oral assessment

(*Continued*)

(*Continued*)

Specialty	Current Exit Examinations/Assessments
Psychiatry	Written assessment: thesis Oral assessment — Paper critique — Case discussion — Topical discussion
Radiation Oncology	FRCR / FRANZCR Part 2
Rehabilitation Medicine	OSCE stations Oral assessment
Renal Medicine	OSCE stations
Respiratory Medicine	MCQs Oral assessment
Rheumatology	Written assessment, including case write up Clinical assessment Oral assessment
Sports Medicine	Paper critique MCQs OSCE stations
Urology	MCQs OSCE stations Oral assessment Exit interview: Research work and logbook review

Exit Criteria from Specialty Training
(Adapted from Ministry of Health Singapore, Specialist Accreditation Board publication on 'Graduate Medical Education in Singapore)[1]

Teaching resources

All sponsoring institutions have various resources to support the training process. These include:

- Structured teaching sessions → didactic teachings, journal club, tumour board discussion, X-ray conference, mortality and morbidity meetings.

- Courses $\rightarrow$ 'Managing Difficult Interactions with Patients', 'Patient Safety Workshop', 'Mastering your risk' and so on
- Journals, books, e-learning resources

Most examples above are illustrated with Otorhinolaryngology simply because it is a specialty that I am more familiar with. However, information regarding all other Specialties is available on their Sponsoring Institution Residency websites:

- NUHS: http://www.nuhs.edu.sg/nuhsresidency/
- Singhealth: http://www.singhealthresidency.com.sg/
- NHG-AHPL: https://www.nhgeducation.nhg.com.sg/nhgresidency

Application

Eligibility criteria

For application to the Residency Programme, eligibility criteria are as below:

- Graduates of Singapore Medical Schools
- Graduates with Primary Medical Qualification registrable under Singapore Medical Council. Graduates with medical qualifications non-registrable under Singapore Medical Council may be considered on a case-by-case basis.
- International Medical Graduates will have to secure an offer of employment as doctor from MOHH or local healthcare institution before they are eligible. For enquiries: physician@mohh.com.sg.
- Certain specialties as detailed above require completion of house officer year/PGY1/Transitional Year before being eligible to apply.

Application timeline

The estimated timeline for Residency application is as below.

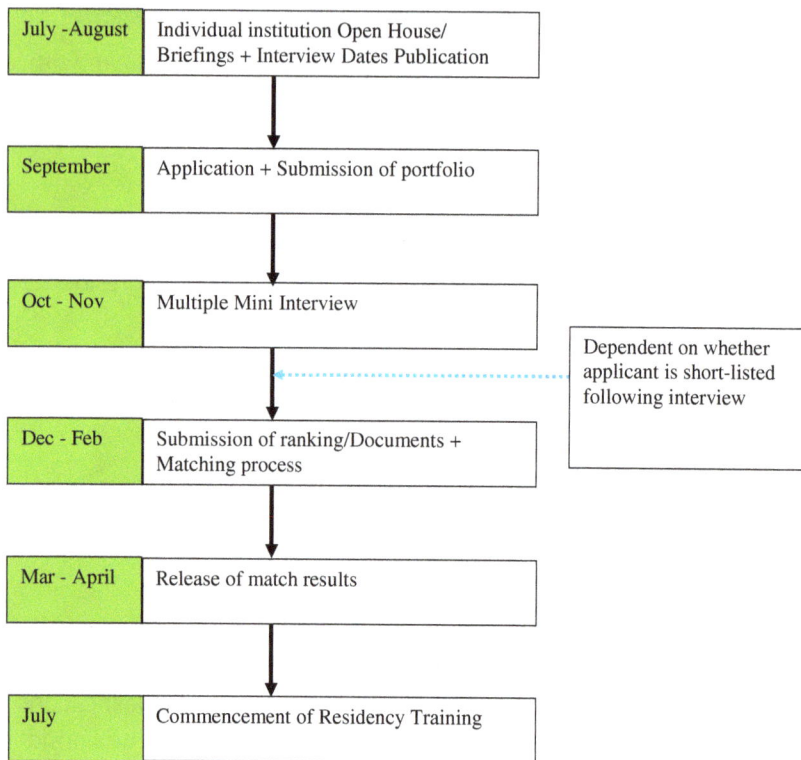

July -August	Individual institution Open House/ Briefings + Interview Dates Publication
September	Application + Submission of portfolio
Oct - Nov	Multiple Mini Interview
Dec - Feb	Submission of ranking/Documents + Matching process
Mar - April	Release of match results
July	Commencement of Residency Training

Dependent on whether applicant is short-listed following interview

Residency Application Timeline.

Application process

- Once application for Residency training opens (usually around September), you can go to the MOH Holdings, Residency website (http://www.physician.mohh.com.sg/medicine/residency/applicationprocess) and submit the application via the 'eResidency' portal.
- First, you need to pre-register by submitting your NRIC or passport number and date of birth.
- For graduating seniors (final-year medical students) from Singapore medical schools or existing house officers and medical

officers, your details are already in the database. Following submission of the information above, a link will then be sent to your NUS or MOH e-mail.

- For all other applicants, the page may say 'applicant not found'. You will have to e-mail physician@mohh.com.sg or jimmy.gan@mohh.com.sg
- You will then need to click on the link in the email to activate your account. This link will lead you to the application form.
- The application form (at the time of writing) consists of sections below:
  - **Personal Details**
  - **Referees**
  - **Portfolio/Resume**
  - **Personal Statement**
  - **Preview + Submit**

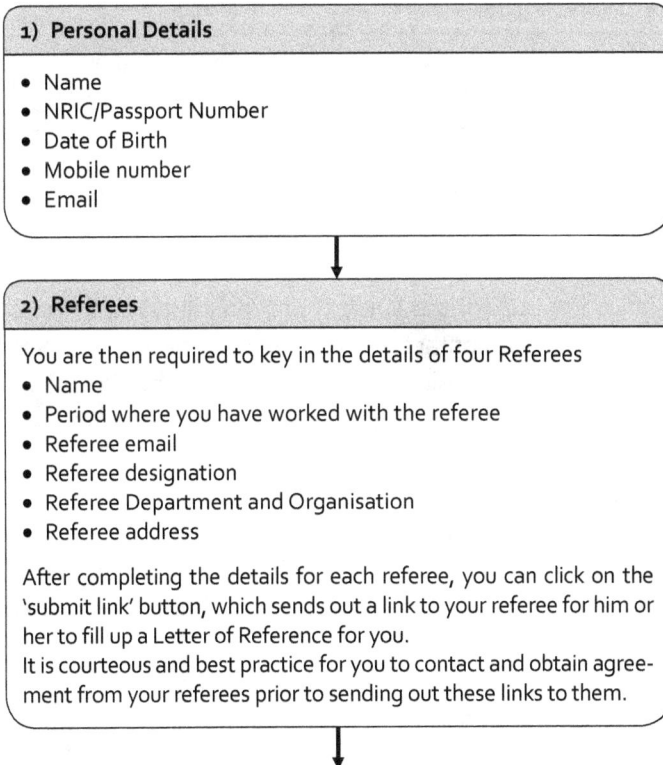

---

1) Personal Details

- Name
- NRIC/Passport Number
- Date of Birth
- Mobile number
- Email

---

2) Referees

You are then required to key in the details of four Referees
- Name
- Period where you have worked with the referee
- Referee email
- Referee designation
- Referee Department and Organisation
- Referee address

After completing the details for each referee, you can click on the 'submit link' button, which sends out a link to your referee for him or her to fill up a Letter of Reference for you.
It is courteous and best practice for you to contact and obtain agreement from your referees prior to sending out these links to them.

3) Portfolio/Resume

- Academic transcripts (upload copies onto the system)
- Academic history (qualifications, institution, year commenced and year completed)
- Elective Postings
- Clinical Rotations completed
- Postgraduate Examinations
- Extra-Curricular Activities/Awards/Accomplishments

4) Personal Statement

Next, you are required to select a programme, e.g. Otorhinolaryngology, and tailor your Personal Statement to the programme you are applying to. There is a limit of 2,000 characters. For more on how to write a Personal Statement, check out Chapter 6 "How to Write Personal Statements."

5) Preview + Submit

Next, you get a preview of your entire form, followed by some terms and condition which you have to agree to in order to submit.

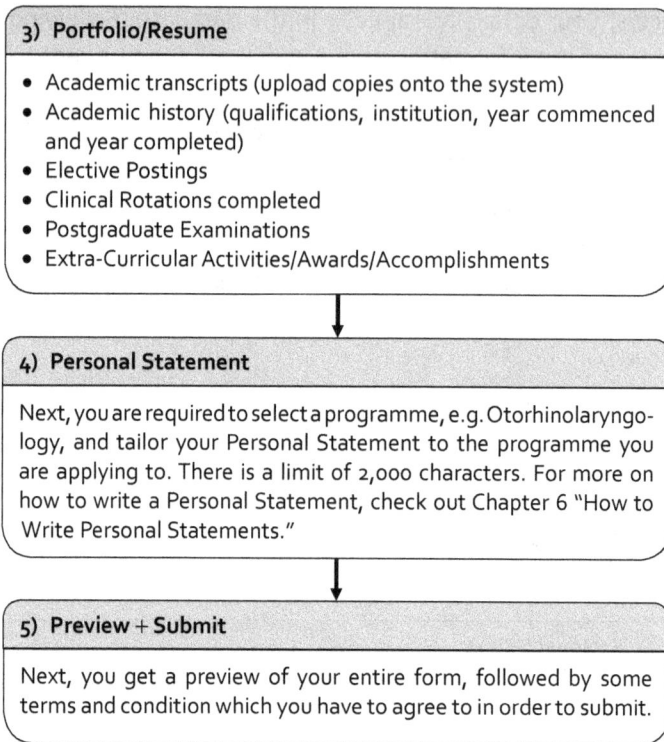

- After submission, you will receive an e-mail confirmation of your submission.
- **Payment.** You will be required to make cheque payment to 'MOH Holdings Pte Ltd' for the application. You are asked to write your name, NRIC and contact number behind the cheque, and also write that it is 'For Residency Application'. At the time of writing, the payment required is SGD $100. Payment can be made online via the application website.
- **Referees.** The onus is upon you to ensure that your referees submit their Letter of Reference for you. You will be able to check the status of their submission when you log into your eResidency account. It will appear as 'Completed' or 'Pending Notification'.
- **Interview.** Shortly after, you will automatically receive an e-mail invitation for the interview. There will be a link in the e-mail

which you can click to book your interview slot. Once your slot is selected, another message will be sent to your e-mail account to confirm your interview timeslot and venue.

- Up-to-date information is available from: http://www.physician. mohh.com.sg/medicine/residency/applicationprocess

Application choices

Each applicant is allowed up to two choices of specialty per Sponsoring Institution. This gives applicants a total of six possible choices of placement. It is advisable that you maximise your chances of success by utilising all six choices.

Submitting ranking + matching process

- Assuming that you are successfully shortlisted after the interview, you will then need to log into your eResidency account again.
- At the eResidency sign-in page, there will be a link for you to click on, which opens up the Ranking form. You will be required to rank a total of six choices from 1 to 6 for your preferred Residency Programme.
- You are allowed to enter fewer than six choices. However, in order to maximise your chances, it is best to fully utilise all six choices.
- Each Residency Programme will also submit their Rank Order List, where they rank the applicants in order of preference.
- A computer algorithm is then used to match applicants' preferences to the Residency Programmes' choices.

Evaluation criteria

Formal evaluation criteria are as below:

- Interview performance and letters of references from referees
- Academic scores
- Student Internship Programme (SIP) performance
- Previous clinical work experience

Other factors that are taken into consideration:

- Work performance in the department
- Applicant's character → Integrity, reliability, diligence, team-working ability, enthusiasm etc. (This is obtained from peers, allied health staff, and senior staff feedback.)
- Research

Training Fees

Successful applicants (Residents) in certain highly subscribed specialties are required to pay a monthly training fee, which amounts to SGD$450 at the time of writing. These specialties include:

- Orthopaedic Surgery
- Ophthalmology
- Otorhinolaryngology
- Obstetrics and Gynaecology
- Plastic Surgery
- Paediatric Medicine
- Dermatology

Application for waiver of this monthly training fee can be done via the MOH Training Award, which has a bond of three years after specialist registration.

What if You Don't Match?

If you did not match successfully, you will then be entered into the House Officer Posting Exercise (HOPEX) or Medical Officer Posting Exercise (MOPEX) for applications into various specialties as a non-trainee.

Switching Tracks/Withdrawal of Application

Successful applicants who withdraw will receive a penalty in which they will not be permitted to apply in the subsequent

Residency application exercise (one-year sit-out). In addition, prior to application to the new programme, the Resident must have withdrawn from their existing programme. An appeal against the penalty can be submitted to the Ministry of Health and will be considered on a case-by-case basis.

In Summary

Despite initial scepticism and resistance, the programme is going from strength to strength. Singapore has adopted the efficiency and structure of the US residency training model whilst retaining some of the favourable features of the old system, creating a unique programme that is tailored to the local context. There are of course aspects which still require improvement. However, directives and resources are being poured in to enhance the quality of training, thus providing a promising future for our postgraduate medical education.

The Residency programme is evolving over the present course. As much as I can illustrate with words, nothing beats seeing/experiencing it first-hand. Come see for yourself, join us on your clinical rotation/attachment/electives, and speak to the residents/faculty/training programme directors during these attachments or open house events to get a better understanding. Here's hoping that you will join us on this journey to produce competent and compassionate specialists to serve the future population of Singapore!

References

1. Specialist Accreditation Board. Graduate Medical Education in Singapore. Ministry of Health Singapore 2018. Available from URL: http://www.healthprofessionals.gov.sg/sab/specialist_training/graduate-medical-education-in-singapore. [Accessed 23/12/18]
2. Cheng CY. Specialist Training in Singapore. Singapore Medical Association 2008. Available from URL: news.sma.org.sg/4001/Training.pdf. [accessed 15/4/2018]

3. Ministry of Health Holdings. Joint Committee on Specialty Training. Ministry of Health Holdings Physician 2018. Available from URL: http://www.physician.mohh.com.sg/specialty_training.html [accessed 15/4/2018]

4. Gan J. eResidency 2018. Ministry of Health Holdings Physician 2018. Available from URL: http://www.physician.mohh.com.sg/residency/downloads/MOHH.pdf [accessed 15/4/2018]

5. Academy of Medicine Singapore. In-Training Examinations. Academy of Medicine, Singapore 2018: Available from URL: http://ams.edu.sg/education-training/in-training-examinations-ites. [accessed 15/4/2018]

6. MOH Holdings. Workplace-Based Performance Assessment (WBA) Reports for Residency Applications. MOH Holdings 2016. Available from URL: http://www.physician.mohh.com.sg/download/WBA.pdf [accessed 15/4/2018]

7. Specialist Accreditation Board. JCST AST BST Seamless Training Requirements. Ministry of Health Singapore 2018. Available from URL: http//www.healthprofessionals.gov.sg/sab/downloads/jcst-ast-seam-less-training-reqirements. [Accessed: 20/12/18]

8. Family Physician Accreditation Board. Route of Entry. Ministry of Health Singapore 2018. Available from URL: http//www.healthprofessionals.gov.sg/fpab/becoming-a-family-physician/entry-criteria-for-family-physician-accreditation/route-of-entry. [Accessed: 20/12/18]

9. Family Physician Accreditation Board. Entry Requirements. Ministry of Health Singapore 2018. Available from URL: http//www.healthprofessionals.gov.sg/fpab/becoming-a-family-physician/entry-criteria-for-family-physician-accreditation/entry-requirements. [Accessed: 20/12/18]

10. Specialist Accreditation Board. Residency Training Programmes. Ministry of Health Singapore 2018. Available from URL: http//www.healthprofessionals.gov.sg/sab/specialist-training/residency-training-programmes. [Accessed: 23/12/18]

11. MOH Holdings. About Residency. MOH Holdings 2018. Available from URL: http://www.physician.mohh.com.sg/medicine/residency/about-residency.

2

The Decision — Which Specialty?

'Doing more things faster is no substitute for doing the right things.'
— Stephen R. Covey

'Four steps to achievement: Plan purposefully. Prepare prayerfully. Proceed positively. Pursue persistently.' — William A. Ward

Key Points

- In considering your subspecialty or career choice, take into account whether you like the core clinical work, how it fits with your personality and life which you envisioned.
- Good ways to find out about the subspecialties include elective postings, clinical rotation, HO or MO postings, research work, Sponsoring Institutions open house events and student interest groups.

- In applying for the subspecialty, it is important to have an awareness of how many posts are up for grabs and where your CV and performance stand amongst all other potential applicants. Comparing your own CV to the previous successful applicants is a useful gauge.
- A reasonably good time to start exploring your career options would be the beginning of fourth year in medical school.
- If you are not able to decide which subspecialty you want to enter as yet, broad base specialties such as Internal Medicine, General Surgery, Anaesthesia and Emergency Medicine will always give you a good broad base experience that can be useful regardless of which specialty you ultimately enter.

Making the decision of which specialty you want to enter and submit the rest of your life to is not easy. It is certainly not a decision to be taken lightly. Truth is, I still do not know how some of my colleagues are able to come to a decision as early as during their medical school years. It took me up to the end of my first medical officer year before I could make up my mind on what I wanted to pursue. Second truth is, I don't regret it. I don't regret spending the time rotating through different specialties, gaining clinical experience and trying my hand on different specialties, having some understanding and exposure to the specialties before ultimately deciding on my final calling.

That is why I do not envy the position of medical students and junior doctors nowadays. Many feel the pressure to decide on their career path early without any prior clinical experience and little exposure. However, given that this is a situation we cannot change, there is not much point bemoaning or debating the effects or discernment of the system. Rather, we could work on what we can do to make the best out of the situation.

Getting to the point — there is no ONE BEST specialty. Each specialty will have its own merits or things that you may like. For instance, Emergency Medicine with its trauma cases and adrenaline rush, Endocrinology with its intellectually challenging complex cases, Surgery with its joy of mastering a technique and alleviating ailments with it, as well as General Practice with its satisfaction in long-term patient care and relations. Equally, within each specialty, there are bound to be something that you might dislike. For instance, Medicine with its lengthy ward rounds and busy calls, Emergency Medicine with its abusers of emergency care services, Neurosurgery with the unrelenting minor head injury admissions, just to name a few.

However, there will be some specialties that are better fit for you than the rest. There should be a few specialties that capture your attention and captivate you sufficiently for you to overcome the annoyances and obstacles along the way. This chapter will bring you through some factors to consider when making this decision, as well as the general flow process leading to the decision. However, do understand that these serve as a general guide. It would be prudent to take these factors into account, but not lose sight of how it fits with other aspects of your life.

Factors to Consider

Below are some factors to consider when making the decision:

1) Do I Like It?
2) How Does It Fit with My Personality?
3) Can I Handle It?
4) What is Life Going to be Like?
5) What are the Career Prospects Like?

1) Do I Like It?

a) *Core clinical work*

Do you like the core clinical work of the specialty? This is fundamental. You need to like the clinical work of the specialty that you choose. There should be something within the core of the specialty that appeals to you, that gives you a sense of fulfilment, something that incites your passion and inspires you. Below are some examples:

- Emergency Medicine — has adrenaline-fuelled trauma/ crash cases requiring quick thinking, teamwork and interaction with various other specialties. It also has a diversity of workload — from simple ailments like cough and cold to unusual presentations like scorpion bites, giving you a wide exposure and promising never to be dull. As one of my ED trainee colleague puts it: 'It's like being a REAL doctor — the type you imagined yourself to be before you get into med school.'

- Renal medicine — allows the development of long-term, fulfilling doctor-patient relationships in chronic care of renal failure patients. It has the challenge of maintaining intricate balance in electrolytes and fluid balance which are important in achieving homeostasis and improving symptoms in patients. Renal Medicine also involves a lot of diagnostic challenge with the systemic and congenital disorders involving the kidneys, which makes it interesting.

- Orthopaedics — has a lot of hands-on work and technical thinking, which can be fun. To devise the best solution given the clinical dilemma (fractured bone) by taking into account the patient's needs (hand dominance, job, daily activities) and biophysics of surgical intervention (plating and screwing) is both mind-stimulating and rewarding.

- Radiology — involves piecing puzzles together and providing diagnosis. Radiologists also have an important role of being a valued member in various multidisciplinary meetings, e.g. aiding in cancer diagnosis and treatment planning in the setting of tumour board. In addition, it has the hands-on option of performing therapeutic procedures in the branch of intervention radiology.

People are generally more satisfied and perform better in a job that interests them. Passion is pivotal, so is realistic expectation. Whilst it is important to ensure you pick something you like, you should also know that it would be naive to expect to be in love with every single part of the specialty. Everyone I know who is passionate about their job still has aspects within their specialty that they dislike. My Emergency Department colleague takes pride in what he does and enjoys sorting out the emergencies that come through the door. Still, at our gathering, we would listen to him recount stories of abusers of the ambulance services, Medical Certificate seekers, and more. Within each specialty, there are bound to be a certain heart sink portion. For instance — ENT with dizziness, Orthopaedics with chronic back pains, Oncology with non-compliant smoking patients, Anaesthesia with chronic pain, just to name a few. But bottomline, if the core clinical work is something that you are passionate about, it will make negating the minor annoyances easier. It will help you keep going at it.

It makes overcoming the minor irritations and periodic exasperations a lot easier.

How to find out more about the specialties?

The process of discovering your interest takes time, experimentation and interaction with the specialties. As per Angela Duckworth in her book "Grit" — passion can be fostered. The initial spark of interest can be cultivated via immersing yourself into the clinical setting of the specialty. Elective postings, clinical rotation, research and attending conferences are good ways of experiencing and discovering more about the specialty.

Given all your busy schedules and the limited time, reading about each specialty is also useful in aiding your decision. There are a few resources below that can give you more insight into the attractions and downside of the specialty, general weekly clinical schedules, subspecialties within the specialty, career path and prospects, tips on how to get in and so on.

- Residency website
  Each institution has its own residency website which gives you an idea of the specialty, the training program, faculty and commitments.
  - https://www.nhgeducation.nhg.com.sg/nhgresidency
  - http://www.singhealthresidency.com.sg/Pages/default.aspx
  - http://www.nuhs.edu.sg/nuhsresidency/

- BMJ Careers
  - ENT: https://www.bmj.com/content/334/7605/s205.2
  - Pathology: https://www.bmj.com/content/338/sbmj.b629
  - Cardiology: https://www.bmj.com/content/351/bmj.h4485

- Royal Colleges websites (e.g. Royal College of Surgeons, Royal College of Physicians, Royal College of Ophthalmology, etc.)
  - https://www.rcophth.ac.uk/wp-content/uploads/2014/07/RCOphth-Ophthalmology-Career-Feb2017.pdf

- Websites for major associations/societies of each specialty (e.g. ENTUK.org, British Cardiovascular Society)
  - E.g. Orthopaedics: http://www.bota.org.uk/

These websites generally provide useful information and guides about each specialty. Admittedly, some of these resources are foreign and hence may not fully reflect the accurate career path, entry requirements and application process for our local setting. However, they will give you a broad overview of the clinical work, characteristics, outlook, manpower trends and clinical issues related to the specialty. This will not only enhance your understanding of the specialty (which will be reflected at the interview) but can also be inspiring and provide a great motivating factor when you can visualize your future better.

Other resources include:

- Career Symposium
  NUS Medical Society organises career talks and sharing session from time to time. They are helpful in providing insight into

various specialties and Residency programme. More information can be obtained from the NUS Medical Society webpage: http://www.nusmedsoc.com/

- Open Houses
  Each Institution (NHG-AHPL, SingHealth, NUHS) holds their own Open House sessions usually around the region of July–August. This is useful in providing information on the training structure and lay-out of each Residency Programme. This also presents an opportunity for interaction with the respective Training Programme Directors for questions regarding training. In addition, Residents in training are usually present. Hence, it is a good opportunity to obtain first-hand information on what training is like, how they got in, what they like about the training/specialty, and what the foreseeable prospects are within the specialty. Dates for the open houses are posted at the MOH physician website: http://www.physician.mohh.com.sg/medicine/residency/about-residency

- Student interest groups
  Student interest groups are great for obtaining more up-to-date specialty-specific information. It is helpful to get on-board these groups which are organised by students for students. These student interest groups often disseminate information via a mailing list. Most will share about specialty-specific events such as conferences, courses and open-houses, in addition to inviting speakers to provide insight into the particular specialty. Some of the local student interest groups have contact via websites (as below). Otherwise, you might be able to find out about these groups during orientation, from your seniors, your medical society committee, or student affairs offices. https://www.duke-nus.edu.sg/education/student-life/student-interest-groups-sig

b) **Do you like the characteristics of the specialty?**

- **Specialist versus Generalist**
  Do you like to know a little about everything? Do you like to know of a wide range of subjects? If so, specialties like Family

Medicine, Emergency Medicine, Geriatrics, Radiology, Pathology and so on, can give you the wide scope that you like. In the world with more and more complex medical problems, doctors with the knowledge breadth are more able to see the connections in the big picture and provide solutions that others might not see.

Conversely, if you prefer to have in-depth knowledge about a specific subject, specialties such as Renal medicine, Dermatology, Cardiothoracic surgery or Neurosurgery may be more suitable.

- **Thinking versus doing**
  If you like thinking and solving complex issues, Endocrinology, Rheumatology or Immunology may be a good choice. If you like hands-on work, Surgery and Interventional Radiology can be very satisfying. If you like a mixture of both, specialties such as Interventional Radiology, Emergency Medicine, Gastroenterology, and Interventional Cardiology can be fulfilling.

- **Patient contact**
  Different specialties offer different amount of patient contact:
  - Long-term care and contact: Family Medicine, Renal Medicine, Endocrinology
  - Short contact: Emergency Medicine, Intensive Care Anaesthesia
  - Minimal contact: Pathology, Radiology

- **What sort of patients do you like?**
  Do you like working with kids? — Paediatrics

  Do you find it fulfilling to doing maternal and child health? — Obstetrics

  Do you like to deal with sick patients? — Anaesthesia, General Surgery, General Medicine, Neurosurgery

  Do you like to deal with generally healthy adults? — Sports Medicine

- **Workload**

  Do you prefer more emergency workload? E.g. Trauma Surgery, Orthopaedics, Cardiology

  Do you prefer more elective workload? E.g. Urology, Ophthalmology, Dermatology, ENT Surgery

- **Mentors and colleagues**

  We are often inspired by role models or the fantastic experience we have during our rotation or attachments with some specialties. This can sometimes be a very powerful motivation. In addition, cultural fit (how you fit with the department) matters. However, you should also be aware that people come and go. Whilst mentors, colleagues and cultural fit are factors for consideration, it is still essential to focus on the fundamentals of each specialty and whether they are a good fit for you.

2) How Does It Fit with My Personality

In essence, having an understanding of your own personality gives you a better idea as to where (which specialties) you fit in. There are various personality tests available (see below), and they serve as **guides** to evaluate potential specialties that suit you. This can help you navigate your career path better as you can leverage on your strengths and put them to good use.

a) Medical Specialty Aptitude Test (MSAT)

This is a set of 130 questions that matches your tendencies to the tendencies of doctors within each specialty. It was developed by Anita Taylor in the book *How to Choose a Medical Specialty*. It asks questions beginning with 'I tend to...' and gives you the ranking of specialties compatible with your character and preferences. Some questions are repetitive. But it doesn't take longer than 10 minutes to complete and my results (see below) were fairly reflective of my current path:

1) Otolaryngology
2) Plastic surgery
3) Ophthalmology

Available from:

- Book by Anita Taylor: 'How to Choose a Medical Specialty'
- www.med-ed.virginia.edu/specialties/TestStructure.cfm

b) **The Pathway Evaluation Program for Medical Professionals**
   This is a similar program that matches your personality profile, values and interests to that of practicing doctors within
   each specialty. This program was developed in 1989 by GSK
   (the pharmaceutical company) and subsequently transferred
   to the Duke University School of Medicine in the United
   States. Responses were collected from 2,407 practicing
   doctors and data was compiled and analysed to create this
   program.

   Available from: http://medweb.usc.edu/pathways/main.
   menu.htm

However, when all is said and done, the personality tests are not
absolute and should be used only as a guide with all other factors
being taken into account. Hence, even if you do not fit into the 'con-
ventional mould' of the specialty, it does not mean you can't do it. It
just means that you need to identify your key talents and be able to
utilise and showcase them within the specialty. It could well be a niche.

3) Can I Handle It?

Be realistic. Do a reasonable assessment of yourself and whether
you are able to handle the different aspects of the specialty.

a) Clinical work
   - Paediatric Surgery — Handling of smaller cavities, smaller
     organs and small patients can be challenging. On top of
     that, skills are required to build rapport with paediatric

patients as well as to deal with parents' emotions/anxieties and to provide reassurance.

- ENT Surgery — Can you handle microscopic/endoscopic work?
- Psychiatry—Requires mental strength, empathy and genuine interest in human behaviour to be able to deal with emotions, mental health, and social circumstances of patients.
- Trauma Surgery — Requires quick thinking/acting/ coordinating skills and the ability to take control under chaotic circumstances.

b) How hard is it to get in?

Needless to say, popular specialties will be more difficult to enter. You need to be aware of how many places are up for grabs and who your competitors are. Do a critical and honest assessment of your own competitiveness. This includes looking at your own CV, past academic performance and general standing among all other potential applicants. Comparing your own CV to those of the successful applicants will be useful as well. Be realistic, but do not deny yourself the chance and oppurtunity.

4) What is Life Going to be Like?

The field of Medicine is notorious for its gruelling hours and unforgiving demands on our lifestyle. The unsociable working hours, frequent on-calls, time needed for research and continued medical education are likely to demand certain compromises of your personal life.

So, do find out more about the specialty — what work demands it has on each level, as a resident, registrar, associate consultant and consultant. This includes:

- number of on-calls + on-call workload
- number of theatre lists
- number of clinic sessions
- ward duties

- teaching commitments
- research sessions
- administrative obligations

In short, you should at least have an idea of what the typical week is like for the resident/registrar/consultant.

At the start of your career, these may not matter as much. However, as obligations increase, there can be various responsibilities competing for your attention. These include work demands, caring for children/spouse/elders, household work, personal development, and so on. Conflict between these obligations can lead to stress and potential burn out. It is therefore important to be aware of these obligations and how they fit in when considering your career choice. Be aware that your priorities are likely to change as you grow older.

In fact, the topic of work-life balance is of such importance that it was actually the subject of one of the questions asked during the Residency Multiple-Mini Interview:

> "If there is an emergency surgery that you have to attend to but it clashes with your son's first birthday party, what would you do?"

These are very real considerations. You have to ask yourself what demands the specialties are likely to make, the implications that the job has on your life, and whether you are prepared to make certain compromises for work.

5) What are the Like? Career Prospects

It is important to evaluate where these career options can bring you and how that fits in with your personal goals.

- Are there research opportunities, opportunities in medical education, opportunities to dabble with technology development?
- Earnings

- Does it fit in with your personal goals — can it help you travel, develop managerial skills
- What is the trend/future development locally — e.g. Radiology may become 24/7, ED and GP skills are more transferrable

General Flow Process on How to Decide

Taking into account other factors mentioned above, below is a guide to a general process of how you could eliminate choices and come to select your specialty of choice.

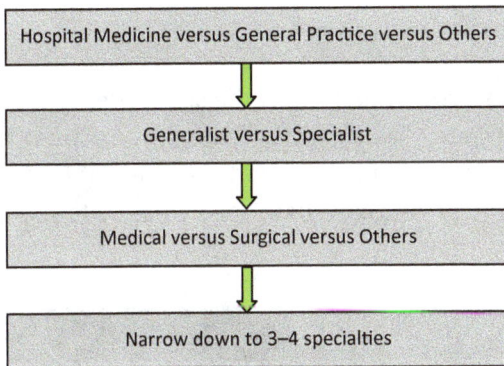

Hospital Medicine versus General Practice versus Others

⬇

Generalist versus Specialist

⬇

Medical versus Surgical versus Others

⬇

Narrow down to 3–4 specialties

Subsequently, have a list of pros and cons of each specialty; weigh it out to see which of those are more important to you.

My own decision process is as follows. I knew I preferred hospital medicine, and I find knowing something in depth more fulfilling. Whilst I enjoyed my medicine postings, I felt Surgery was a better fit with my personality. In addition, I knew I wanted to have a balanced life outwith my medical career. So I actively requested for 2 postings — ENT Surgery and Urology for my 1st Medical Officer Year. After going through both postings, I went with ENT Surgery.

Quick Hacks?

If you are too lazy to go through these factors one by one, an easy and useful way out is to speak to those who are in the specialties. Speak to residents, registrars, consultants and ask them about:

a)   What made them choose their specialty
b)   What do they like about it
c)   What do they dislike about it
d)   What is their typical work week like

A good time to ask is when you are at your electives/ attachments/rotations. Based on the answers you get from various people, you can get an idea of:

- What's good or bad about the specialties
- Which are the factors that the doctors place more importance on and how they are relevant to you
- A gauge of which of these specialties suits you best

When Should I Decide?

It is understandable why some medical students feel the pressure to decide early on their specialty of choice. To decide early during medical school years has its advantages. It allows time for directed effort in preparation of the CV, hence increasing the chances of being successful in securing a place in the Residency Programme. CV preparation takes time.

However, the flip side of the coin is, without the time and enough clinical experience, some may make hasty, ill-informed decisions which they may regret later. Given the limitation of time and the current situation, I propose that the beginning of the fourth year in medical school is a good time to start actively exploring your options.

By the fourth year, you would have gone through some clinical rotations and electives to give you *some* idea of what you might like.

It also gives you a bit more time to decide on your further electives, where you could direct them and do them in the specialties that you think you might want to join. This also gives you some time to do your clinical research. It takes time for research planning, ethics approval, data collection and write-up. Hence, sometimes, it can take up to over a year for publications to materialise.

If you are a HO/MO, don't worry, it is never too late. As I said, it took me up to the end of my first MO year to make up my mind. It means you would have more breadth of experience and have an even better idea of what suits you and what doesn't. But do start making concentrated effort towards the specialty(ies) of your choice.

Can't Decide?

If you are unsure or cannot make up your mind, it is okay. Take time to explore, but be purposeful in each step that you take. What this means is, each career decision/step you make should be directed towards helping you make a decision.

To illustrate further, this means, when you apply for MOPEX rotation, you should be applying to the few specialties (assuming you have already narrowed down your choices) that you think you might be interested in. This will allow you to immerse yourself in the clinical work of that specialty, and in doing so, find out more about the ins and outs of the specialty to see if it interests you. This will also allow contact with the residents/registrars/consultants of the specialty, whom you could ask about the respective specialty.

Alternatively, go through some other rotations which are likely to benefit you no matter what specialty you ultimately end up choosing. For instance, as a medical student and HO, I enjoyed Respiratory Medicine but I still liked doing things with my hands. When I could not make up my mind as to which specialty to enter, I applied for ICU rotation (in UK) for my medical officer year, as I knew regardless of whether I land a career in Medicine or Surgery, a posting in ICU would still be beneficial from both clinical experience and CV building viewpoint. In general, specialties like Emergency Medicine, Anaesthesia, Radiology, Internal Medicine, and General Surgery are good for broad base experience and can be useful regardless of the specialty you ultimately enter. For instance, if you did General Medicine but ultimately decide to go into Orthopaedics, you could say you actively chose a General Medicine rotation to as it equips you with the ability to initiate management on the acute medical problems in orthopaedic patients. Or if you did Anaesthesia and want to enter Internal Medicine, you could say the Anaesthesia rotation allowed you to acquire skills including intubation, setting lines, and managing acutely ill patients, which are valuable skills for an Internal Medicine trainee.

In addition, try and link up with the departments and get some research projects going. This will also give you some exposure to the clinical work, and at the same time increase your 'visibility' within the department, and hence, should you choose to do that specialty ultimately, you stand a better chance of being successful in the selection.

Ideally, given the level of competition in the current climate, you should be doing research in the specialty that you want to enter. After all, having a publication/presentation/research in the specialty demonstrates your intent and strong interest in the specialty. However, if you can't decide on which specialty, one trick is to do projects that have a general or double theme, even better if it could be themed in the two specialties you want to enter. For instance:

1) Incidence of postoperative pulmonary embolism (Radiology, Internal Medicine, Surgery)
2) Fall (Orthopaedics, Geriatrics)
3) Dizziness (ENT, Neurology, Internal Medicine)

So hopefully, until you make up your mind, you could continue working towards enhancing your CV.

Made a Choice but Regret It Now?

This is understandable and easy to empathise with, given that the current Residency system tends to channel doctors into various specialties early in the career. Hence, sometimes decisions are made from a myopic view and may not have been thoroughly thought out/trialled out.

It is never too late to change. Better now than being stuck doing something that you do not like for the rest of your life. The flip side of the coin is that the Residency Programme enforces a penalty for switching tracks — the applicant is not allowed to apply for the next one year. In addition, if you keep changing career paths, your commitment and decision-making ability become questionable to future selectors. Hence, do make sure that you have thought it out thoroughly and understand why you absolutely do not want to continue training in the specialty. Also, you should start thinking about the options of what else you want to do.

Good news is that the MOH Residency website does state that they will consider if you have 'exceptional grounds and reasons for change' (http://www.physician.mohh.com.sg/medicine/residency/faqs). So, it might be an idea to write in to appeal your case and hopefully negate the one-year penalty. Moreover, whichever rotation that you have done is never wasted. It gives you more breadth of experience and useful skills to bring into the new specialty that you choose to enter.

In Summary

The truth is, your priorities will continuously evolve. What's important to you now may change 10 years down the road. So, as of all things in science when there are no definite answers, your best bet would be to make your decision or best educated guess based on the most exhaustive and comprehensive information at hand.

3

Preparation of CV

"The secret of getting ahead is getting started." — Mark Twain

Key Points

- CV is a demonstration of your achievements, intent and interest for the specialty that you intend to apply into.
- Common headings of CV include: Personal Details, Undergraduate and Postgraduate Qualifications, Prizes and Awards, Memberships, Previous Employments, Publications, Presentations, Courses and Conferences Attended, Teaching Experience, Key Skills, Personal Statement and Referees.
- Taking the time now to write and review your CV will give you the opportunity to identify any gaps in your experience and therefore gives you the time to work on it or respond to opportunities that arises.
- CV preparation takes time, presentations/publications take time to materialise, courses only happen on limited dates and skills require time to develop. So, do get started early.

Curriculum vitae (CV) preparation has become increasingly important in the setting of Residency training, where potential candidates may be selected straight from medical school for the job without having worked with the department. Your CV is a demonstration of your achievements, ability, diligence, decision-making capability, organisational skills, as well as your intent and interest. It may help give a favourable first impression to your selectors. In addition, when deciding between applicants of similar clinical calibre for a Residency post, a good CV can help you stand out.

CV writing and CV preparation are different things. CV writing is the design and presentation of your existing portfolio to convince your selectors that you are the right candidate for the job. CV preparation, however, is the effort in developing items on your CV (clinical skills, work experience, research, presentations, examinations, etc.). As implied, this takes much more effort and careful consideration.

At the time of writing, the initial application to a Residency Programme does not require a submission of a physical copy of the CV. It requires, however, submission of a 'Portfolio', which is similar to a CV. It requires details such as qualification, work experience, achievements, referee and so on. Subsequently, if you are then short-listed for the institution matching exercise, most institutions will request a copy of your CV.

This chapter aims to provide you with an idea of how a CV should be structured, and hopefully to help you identify the gaps in your CV and guide you towards developing the items in your CV.

Timing — When is a Good Time to Start Preparing

As alluded to earlier in Chapter 2, intentional or not, the current system favours people who make up their mind early. The earlier you make up your mind, the higher the chance you can utilise and maximise the opportunities that the medical school provides to develop your CV. By this I mean purposefully planning your clinical rotations, electives, research projects, attending career symposiums or being part of the specialty-specific student interest group.

As proposed earlier, I think the beginning of the fourth year is a good time to start. This is because by then you would have gone through some clinical rotations to have an idea of what you like or dislike. Moreover, you have a choice of further electives to reaffirm your choice or to help you reconsider. In addition, it still gives you sufficient time to develop your CV.

If you are a house officer or medical offficer, don't worry. It is never too late to start. You need to see the advantage you have over medical students — you have clinical experience behind you to guide your career choice. Your work and clinical performance adds confidence for your selection panel. In addition, the rapport and proximity you have with the department gives you first-hand information that can aid in obtaining a research project or for application to a MOPEX rotation. That said, do get started and capitalise on what you have.

CV Structure

There are a variety of ways to structure one's CV. Frankly there is no one best structure. You can include or exclude whichever headings as long as you ensure that it is relevant, truthful and aligns with what your interviewers/selection panel are looking for. One of my Professor in Edinburgh once told me that he has a few versions of his CV, each tailored for different purposes. Below is a guide. Apart from the headings, do take notice of the sequence in which it is laid out. The sequence should highlight the most impressive item but at the same time follow a logical order.

1. **Cover page**
    - This is optional, but personally I feel it gives your CV a more professional appearance

- You should print your name and qualifications — MBBS, MRCS, etc.

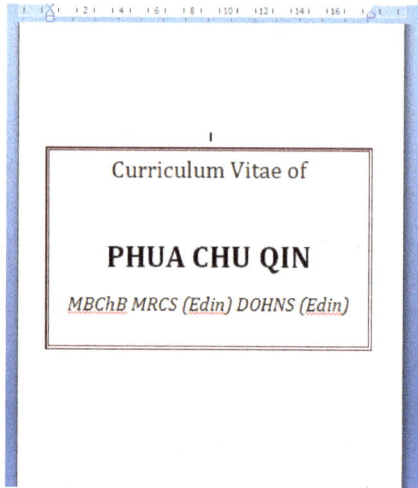

2. Contents page

- This is optional. It can be useful if you have a lot of pages in your CV

Contents

	Item	Page
1	Personal Details	3
2	Undergraduate Education	3
3	Postgraduate Examinatins and Qualifications	3
4	Prices and Awards	3
5	Memberships	3
6	Previous Employment	3
7	Publications	4
8	Research in Progress	5–6
9	Poster Presentation	6
10	Oral Presentation	7
11	Courses Attended	8–12
12	Teaching Experience	12–13
13	Key Skills	13
14	Medical Electives	14
15	Personal Statement	14
16	Referees	15

3. **Personal details**
   - Name
   - Date of birth
   - IC number
   - SMC registration
   - Address
   - E-mail
   - Phone number

4. **Qualification and examinations** (+ year achieved):
   - Undergraduate: MBBS
   - Postgraduate: MRCS, MRCP, MRCOG, etc.

5. **Prizes, grants, scholarships**
   - I group them together in my own CV because I do not have very many of them
   - Feel free to use these as separate headings
   - However, I think this should be presented early in your CV because these are achievements that are worth highlighting to your selection panel

6. **Memberships**
   - Student council memberships, society memberships, Royal College memberships, etc.

7. **Work experience/employment history**
   - Useful to include:
     - Work period (e.g. Jan 2011–June 2011)
     - Department
     - Post held (house officer, medical officer, etc.)
   - It usually looks more organised to present this information in a table format.
   - In terms of order of presentation — whether to put the most recent post first or to have it in a chronological order, it does not quite matter. You can sometimes manoeuvre this to your advantage. For instance, if you are applying for a job in

General Surgery and your most recent jobs happened to be surgical postings, then I would put the most recent jobs on top.

8. **Research and publications**
   - I personally prefer to separate the headings into 'Publications' and 'Research in Progress' for the sake of clarity
   - In terms of order of presentation — whether to put the most recent qualification or the earliest achieved first — again, it does not quite matter. However, you should try to be consistent throughout your CV. For example, if you have chosen to present items in a chronological order starting from the most recent item under 'Employment history', you should follow the same sequence under 'Research and Publications' and for the rest of the CV.

9. **Presentations**
   - Oral Presentations + Poster presentations
   - Do include:
     - Topic of presentation
     - Conference
     - Date presented
     - Optional: audience present, e.g. presented to members of the American Society of Laryngology

10. **Courses and conferences**
    - Do include:
      - Course/Conference title
      - Date

11. **Teaching experience**
    - Do include:
      - Topic taught, event organised
      - Date
      - Audience
      - Optional: You can include 'Objective', e.g. Objective of the teaching session was to assist final-year medical students in preparation for their final examination.

- o Optional: You can also include 'Role', e.g. were you a tutor, or were you one of the organisers for an event, what were you in-charge of doing?
- o Try to avoid being too wordy though

12. Electives
- Do include:
  - o Specialty
  - o Hospital/venue of electives
  - o Date
  - o Optional: You can include objective of electives, e.g. to gain exposure to the different end of the disease spectrum in a Third World country and learned to work under limited resources.

13. Key skills
- This could be any skills relevant to the post you are applying to, e.g. clinical skills, language skills, team working skills, computer skills, etc.

KEY SKILLS	
Surgical Skills	• Tonsillectomy • Grommet Insertion • Manipulation of Fractured Nose • Septoplasty • Pharyngosocpy • Excision of Simple Ear Lesions • Excision of Simple Nose Lesions • Sinus Surgery: Uncinectomy, Anterior and posterior ethmoidectomy
Clinical Skills	• ENT Skills: microsuction of ears, drainage of peritonsillar abscess, nasal packing, nasal cautery, naso-endoscopy, rigid endoscopy • Basic Life Support • Advanced Life Support • Central Line Insertion • Arterial Line Insertion • 3-way catheter and suprapubic catheter insertion • Lumbar puncture • Ascitic tap
Team Working Skills	• Committee Member of University Halfway Ball
Language & Dialects	• Read, write and speak : English, Mandarin, Malay, Cantonese, Hokkien

14. Extra-curricular activities
- E.g. charity work, expeditions, interests

15. Personal statement
- State your interests, profile, goals and how they aligns with the job

16. Referees
- Name of referees
- Position of employment of the referees
- E-mail, contact number, address

Taking time now to write and review your CV gives you the opportunity to identify any gaps (e.g. lack of publication, exams, courses, etc.) in your experience and therefore gives you time to work on it/ respond to opportunities that arise before the application process starts.

Working Towards Each Item of CV — How to Maximise Yield

Now that you have an idea of how the CV can be structured, you should be able to identify any gaps present. The next step would be to work and develop those items on your CV. Below are a few things which you could work on.

1) Postgraduate examinations
- Postgraduate examinations such as the MRCP and MRCS are widely accepted milestones that provide evidence that you have what it takes (clinical knowledge, skills and attributes) to progress in your advanced medical or surgical training.

- Generally, these examinations are formidable undertakings. They take time, a lot of effort and money. Yet they can provide reassurance to your selectors that you are 'academically fit' in the pursuit of a Residency career, and it tells them that you are definitely interested enough to make such a commitment.

- Timing: One consideration is when best to sit for the examinations. Generally part A of MRCS and part I MRCP are MCQs or Best of Fives. Therefore they can theoretically be taken at any time. Undoubtedly, having clinical experience helps. Most people I know sat for MRCS part A between the end of House Officer year to year 1–2 of Medical Officer year. For MRCP part I, the MRCP UK website states that people have the highest pass rates when they sit for it 12–24 months post graduation.[1]

- Eligibility criteria — Do take note that some of these postgraduate examinations may require some clinical work experience for one to be eligible. For instance, MRCP part 1 requires at least 12 months of medical employment. To be eligible to sit for the MRCS, you need a medical degree which is recognised by the College. So, be sure to get up to date information from the Royal Colleges/Examinations websites.

- Also note that there are limited attempts (six attempts for each part of the MRCP and MRCS) and a limited eligibility period to move on to next part of the examination (e.g. from MRCP part 2 needs to be taken within seven years of passing MRCP part 1).

- For other postgraduate examinations, e.g. Anaesthesia, Radiology, Ophthalmology, it's best to ask seniors within the specialty as to when best to take the examinations. Most of these are difficult and require a certain amount of clinical exposure.

- Duration of study preparation — anything from 1–6 months.

- Practical tips: Partner up with another person who is also sitting for the examination, obtain and share resources.

    o Question bank — Locally, there are past-year questions which are passed down from seniors to juniors. Do ask your seniors who have just sat for the examinations — most are more than willing to pass on the information.

    o Anatomy teaching at National University Singapore (NUS) — If you have a group, you can try asking the anatomy professors at NUS for a teaching session. In fact, most of them organise sessions from time to time. This is particularly useful for passing the MRCS.

    o Share online questions — I passed my MRCS part A by doing online questions and studying the answers. 'OnExamination' and 'PasTest' (links below) have very extensive and comprehensive question banks. Before you sign up for any of these, it would be helpful to make sure that the question formats are in line with the examination format (e.g. MCQ or best of fives or single best answers). http://www.onexamination.com http://www.pastest.co.uk

    o Ask for practical teaching/mock exam sessions from clinical doctors. When I was doing my General Surgery posting at Tan Tock Seng Hospital (TTSH), the General Surgery Registrars were extremely good (both in enthusiasm and in being substantial) at providing teaching for MRCS preparation.

    o Likewise, the General Medicine team in TTSH have been known to organise prep sessions for the MCRP.

    o Below are the websites with information for the MRCP and MRCS. They are useful to check for syllabus and format, examination dates and venues, eligibility criteria, sample questions, fees etc. http://www.mrcpuk.org/Pages/Home.aspx http://www.intercollegiatemrcsexams.org.uk/

2) Prize/grants/scholarships

- Prizes/grants/scholarships are usually awarded on a competitive basis and often require a certain amount of rigour and academic excellence. They thus lend credibility, exposure and prestige to their recipients.

- So I would say, keep an eye out for these; if the opportunity arises, go give it a try. But if you don't get it — don't lose sleep over it. Take it in stride knowing that, really, these are in no way any reflection of what sort of doctor you are or are going to be.

- Below are some resources. Generally, medical school administrative offices have a list of awards/grants/scholarships. The rest are usually available on Medical Society/Royal College websites. Locally, the Singapore Health and Biomedical Congress (SHBC) hands out research award which comes with prize money. They have specific categories for student as well as junior doctors, which makes it slightly more attainable.

  http://www.nus.edu.sg/admissions/undergrad/scholarships/freshmen/scp/scholarship-scp-nus-undergraduate.html
  http://nusmedicine.nus.edu.sg/graduatestudies/awards-prizes
  http://www.shbc.com.sg
  https://www.rcsed.ac.uk/professional-support-development-resources/grants-jobs-and-placements/research-travel-and-award-opportunities/student-bursaries

3) Employment history

- Given the limited time for you to build your CV towards the Residency application, careful planning of your HOPEX/MOPEX postings is extremely important to give you the advantage. It will also demonstrate foresight and prudent planning in steering your career.

- This is something which can give you the most leverage in your career navigation. There are few strategies you could apply, which include:
  - o Rotation through the specialty which you hope to apply for in Residency
  - o Rotation through other relevant specialties
  - o Rotation through specialties with general themes.

- Rotation through THE specialty: Obtaining a HOPEX/MOPEX rotation in the specialty (and ideally the institution) you intend to enter will give you significant advantage over those who have not rotated through the department.

- A few advantages of rotating through the specialty of your choice
  - o It gives you the chance to immerse yourself in the clinical work. This is your chance to assess whether the clinical work in that specialty is something you enjoy and can continue doing for the rest of your career. It also gives you the first-hand experience of the workload, daily operations and culture of the specialty/department. This can be useful in assessing whether a career in that specific specialty is suitable for you.

  - o Furthermore, spending time in the department gives you 'face time'. It gives you the opportunity to increase your visibility as a favourable candidate for the job. Once in the department, you have the opportunity to impress your selectors by showcasing your work ethics, clinical acumen and knowledge.

  - o It gives your selectors/bosses the chance to know you and to assess you in person. This tends to give them more confidence in selecting you as a resident.

  - o The close proximity you have with the department allows you to obtain research projects and a platform to present your research.

o In addition, it puts you in the vantage point of being in the know about the latest happenings. For instance, you might be more aware of the resident intake, the number of competitors and whether your application is favourable.

o Members of the department can also become your referee for the Residency application.

- HOPEX/MOPEX places get filled up really quickly in some specialties. To increase your chances of getting a rotation in the specialty, it would be useful to get in touch with the head of department (HOD) or programme director (PD) to express your interest before the applications start.

- It would be useful to email the HOD/PD your CV and state your intention of joining the department as a HO/MO (the e-mail address is usually available on hospital sites, in journals, or alternatively, call hospital switchboard — ask for the department secretary number and then obtain the HOD e-mail via the secretary).

- If it is feasible, it would be even better if you could meet the HOD/PD in person to discuss the possibility of obtaining a HOPEX/MOPEX rotation with the department. Although this can be difficult sometimes owing to busy schedules, it is worth making the effort. This is because it demonstrates sincerity and effort, and it might help the HOD/PD remember you better.

- Most HODs are quite kind in that they will let you know if they are likely to be able to take you in for the next posting. If they do agree to take you in, it is always useful to send a reminder e-mail closer to the MOPEX application date.

- Once you get in, it is important to make on-going efforts develop your career. Some people get into a rotation in the department and then sort of lose sight of what they are trying to achieve. This is mostly because clinical duties can be taxing and consuming. Balancing career development, academic demands and clinical duties can be challenging and it is easy to let time pass by.

- Rightfully, your priority should be to execute your clinical duties well. However, it is also important that you manage your time effectively such that you still have time to demonstrate that you are a favourable candidate. Time in the department is invaluable in helping you consolidate your clinical experience and gain good opinions. If done right, it can have a significant impact on your career prospects.

- Therefore, it helps to be proactive and organised to make the most out of a rotation. For instance, prior to the start of the rotation, it is worth contacting the MOs/Residents currently in the rotation to gain insight to what lies ahead. This allows understanding of requirements of clinical duties, estimation of workload and planning for potential research projects. This knowledge therefore allows better time management and preparation for the rotation.

- It is useful to set up a meeting with your supervisor at the beginning of the rotation to discuss your aims and objectives. Lay out what you need and want to achieve to help you get that Residency job and seek help from your supervisor in achieving this.

- Be solid in your clinical work. Demonstrating competency in your day-to-day work and showing good work ethics often improves your 'desirability' as it gives your selectors the reassurance that should you get that residency post, you will ease into it with no problems. This usually requires regular reading and active efforts to learn.

- The rotation should also be utilised to the maximum for things to do, e.g. research, audit, presentations in addition to gaining clinical experience. However, be realistic about the timeframe. Six months can be short if you are aiming for a randomised controlled trial or doing a project that requires ethics or funding approval. Asking to join an existing project or doing a retrospective study might be more realistic. Alternatively, you should try and get started with the project before the rotation starts or be prepared to continue on even after the rotation ends.

- Team players who are able to put aside differences for a common goal are always highly valued. It is important to align with department/team's cause. It would be helpful if you could offer to do work and share out team responsibilities even when it is not within your job scope. Do step up when it is required, but at the same time be mindful not to overstep boundaries.

- Rotation through OTHER RELEVANT specialties: Certain specialties are extremely popular and can be difficult to get into. So if you are unable to get into the specialty of your choice, there are usually other relevant specialties that you can try to swap into.

- Diversifying your experience in various other relevant specialties can be favourable as it means you will be equipped to work in a multidisciplinary setting and you will be able to bring in different skill sets to your chosen specialty.

- To illustrate, if you are trying for a Dermatology job, having a rotation in Rheumatology is often useful as it allows exposure to connective tissue disorders, which is often managed in a multidisciplinary fashion by Dermatologist and Rheumatologists.

- Other examples:
  For ENT: Neurosurgery, Plastic Surgery
  For Orthopaedics: Hand Surgery, Trauma Surgery (General Surgery), Radiology

- Rotation through GENERAL specialties: If you are undecided, specialties with general themes are useful. As alluded to earlier, these include Emergency Medicine, Internal Medicine, Radiology, Anaesthesia, General Surgery, etc.

- These specialties are useful in helping you consolidate your basic medical practices and get comfortable with management of patients.

- If you are early in your career (House Officer year or first Medical Officer year), it is worth getting into busy rotations such as Internal Medicine or General Surgery. This can accelerate your learning curve — how to manage sick patients, how to make referrals, how to pre-round/round effectively, how to use the computer system, how to prioritise and to manage time, as well as how to work in teams. These skills will come in handy when you ultimately get into your specialty of choice, as it can help showcase your efficiency and time-management skills and at the same time allow you to focus more of your effort in career development.

- The reality is — you will not always get the posting that you want. In which case, it is then up to you to 'sell' to your interviewers/selectors on how whichever posting you did get has equipped you better for the upcoming Residency post.

- E.g. for an Orthopaedic Residency applicant, posting through Radiology will have helped with better understanding of indications for scans, procedure of the scans and skill set in interpretation of in the ordering of scans and reading of scans, which will come in handy during day-to-day work in Orthopaedics. Likewise, a stint in Rehabilitation Medicine allows familiarisation with multidisciplinary work and understanding of the downstream recovery process, which undoubtedly will help with organising care for Orthopaedic patients in the future.

- 'Taster week' — Taster week or job shadowing was a concept that was very prevalent when I was in the UK. The concept is not new to Singapore. It is essentially a short attachment to the department (in the capacity of an observer) — anything ranging from 2–14 days or more to give you insight to the specialty and gain some clinical exposure. It is similar to the electives that medical students do, or the sort of short attachment that overseas graduates come for in their own time during their holidays. If you are not able to get a rotation in the department, sometimes taster week can be useful.

- Traditionally, 'taster weeks' are meant for you to explore in detail the clinical work or day-to-day operations of the specialty to help make your career choice. However, it can also be a means for you to spend some time with the current trainees or consultants to enquire about the career pathway, entry into the specialty, and how the career choice was made.

- It can also be a stepping stone to future opportunities (e.g. getting a MOPEX rotation in the department).

- Unfortunately, this has to be done on your own time — usually your own annual leave. In addition, it is more difficult to leave an impression over such a short duration.

- However, the short duration of the attachment makes it manageable because it is likely that you will be able to afford the time. In addition, there are usually no limitations or restricted dates of when you can do the attachment as long as you can ensure that your own clinical duties are covered and that the department of your choice is happy to take you on.

- This takes pre-planning and it is important that you help sort out the any paperwork that is required (annual leave application, application for attachment, etc.).

4) **Research and publications**
   - Practical tips on how to develop research projects and achieve publications will be covered in detail in Chapter 4: Research and Publications

   - Essentially there are few things you need to be aware of:
     o Research and publications are persuasive components which can improve your chances in getting a Residency job because it demonstrates your commitment to the specialty, interest and ability.

- o Research and publications take time to materialise, hence get started early
- o General workflow: find a mentor → get a project →sort out ethics application (if required) → data collection + data entry → data analysis → write up → submission for publication

- The process can take anything from months to years

- Practical tips for making this process easier:
  - o Find a good mentor
  - o Ask to join an existing project
  - o Try to choose projects (if you have the choice) which are manageable and achievable in the limited timeframe that you have. For instance, projects which require a long duration for subject recruitment or projects that are still waiting for funding may be better left for the future.

5) **Presentations: Oral and poster**
- Presentations are important items on the CV. The impact of presentations is two-fold. First, as an item on the CV, it is evidence that you have completed the loop of the research and have disseminated the results. In addition, when you present your research to the department or at a conference that is attended by Seniors from the specialty, it can help leave a favourable impression.

- Practical tips on how to do oral presentations are covered in Chapter 5: How to do Presentations.

- There are various platforms for presentations, including departmental journal club/research meetings, local conferences, regional and international conferences.

- Most people overlook the advantage of doing presentation in a local setting. Whilst it can sound impressive having a line on the CV that says 'Presented poster at the American Academy of Otolaryngology Head and Neck Surgery Annual

Meeting 2013', presenting a paper in a local conference, ideally one where most of your future selection panel/consultants in the specialty are likely to attend, can be beneficial. For one, it can be an opportunity for the consultants to know your work, form a good impression and hopefully one that is lasting enough during the selection process.

- In addition, many of these local conference are organized by local hospital departments. Presenting your paper at the local conference can help show your support, not to mention the fact that you will be able to stay in-tune with the latest clinical development of the specialty from the viewpoint of the local setting. For some of the major local conferences such as the Singapore Health & Biomedical Congress, some of the hospitals do take into account the number of submissions from each department. Hence, submitting your work can also be a form of support.

- Some general tips, prior to submitting your work, always first check and obtain approval from your supervisor of your project/paper. In addition, when at these conferences, do try and mingle and talk to the residents/registrars/consultants of the specialty. It can be helpful to introduce yourself and let them know of your interest in the specialty. No harm striking up conversation about the presentations that the Consultants/Residents/Registrars are doing at the conference (usually it will be stated in the programme book), or just ask for information about entry into the specialty such as number of places, competition, what you can be doing to increase your chances of entering, and so on. Again, this is helpful to help leave them with an impression of you.

- To get an idea of which conferences are good to submit your paper to, you can ask your supervisor, or current Residents/Registrars/MOs in the specialty. They usually receive email circulation about local and overseas meetings, and are therefore more in-tune and up-to-date with which meetings or conference are good to attend, and which ones would allow you to present your research.

- If done well, a good local presentation can also lead to further research opportunities or clinical rotation.

- Hence, actively seek out the platforms for presentations. It usually helps if you have a good mentor to help you seek out these opportunities.

6) Electives

- From the viewpoint of career development, electives are for you to learn about the specialty, gain clinical exposure, make contact and hopefully leave a good impression.

- To maximise yield from your electives, have ample time to learn and explore the specialty. Take note of the patients and illnesses you encounter, the typical schedule of a Resident/Registrar/Consultant (number of theatre sessions, clinics, ward work), the settings in which you are expected to work (outpatient, theatre, outreach/community visits), skill sets required (communication in palliative care, surgical skills, organisation skills), demands and challenges of the specialty, workload (hours, how many patients you see a day), what you enjoyed most, what you disliked, and how does your personality and aptitude fit with the specialty. Speak to residents about entry requirements, get a feel of how competitive it is to get in, ask for any advice for medical students/applications.

- However, try not to forget that electives can also be one of the highlights of your medical school years, and possibly a memorable and life-defining experience, one that you will remember for years to come. So whilst the paragraphs below are pointers on how to maximise your learning during electives from a career development viewpoint, I would still advocate that you avoid taking a too myopic view and focus too much on career development. So for instance, if you have a chance of doing an elective in a local department where you know will increase the department's exposure to you and increase your chances into Residency, versus that of an elective in another country such as India/Africa doing work that is not related to specialty that you intend to apply to, I would urge you to consider the latter if your situation allows. The exposure to a different healthcare environment and experience will enrich you as a healthcare provider and make you a more balanced individual, which are valuable in your future practice of medicine.

- To make the most out of your elective, the first thing you should do is to always introduce yourself to the most senior person in the room/OT/rounds/clinic (as well as other team members). Let them know your name, how long you are attached to the unit for and, if possible, what you want to learn during the elective.

- Most of you are too polite to interrupt in case you appear intrusive or obstructive. If you are lucky, sometimes your supervisor or the department secretary will introduce you to the team, but more often than not, this does not happen and you will need to do it yourself. It can be awkward at times because you need to find the right time to 'abruptly' introduce yourself. Trust me, that short spurt of awkwardness is worth bearing.

- Do this as early as possible (rather than just pitch up at the rounds daily and follow around quietly) because it helps build rapport and often opens up opportunity for the team to get you involved in their work or to teach you.

- Next, try and get more involved. Many elective students tend to be rather passive in that they sit quietly in clinic or stand quietly aside during rounds or in OT. I understand the dilemma of not wanting to get in the way. However, you risk become forgettable, which does not help if you are hoping for a Residency job in that specialty. There are lots of ways to be helpful, such as opening the doors for the patients as they come in, or helping the old patient onto the examination couch, or handing tissues to patients when they cry, and many more.

- In my own clinic setting, I certainly find it easier to ask patients for permission for students to history or examine them when students take such initiatives. It is easier for me to introduce you as part of our team.

- If you are not sure what to do, one way is to introduce yourself to the doctor/nurse/allied health whom you are attached to and ask how you can be of help.

- In a surgical attachment, when in OT, a basic courtesy is to introduce yourself to the lead surgeon when you enter.

- Ask to scrub in whenever you can. You always get a much better view. Plus if you are scrubbed, there is a higher chance of getting to do something (often not a lot, but at least the possibility is there). However, do try and have the EQ to gauge when to ask and when not to ask. It would be inappropriate to ask to scrub if you do not have hospital clearance to scrub for the posting. Other situations to avoid asking is when it is a case where the patient is critically unwell, or when the surgeon is in the midst of a difficult manoeurve. Also, if the answer is a 'no', try to be understanding and not get upset. Sometimes, there may be a lot of people scrubbed and insufficient space. Or it could simply be the surgeon's preference. Hey, again, at least you tried. It is always worth a try.

- Try and learn about the patient cases by reading up the case files of the ward patients in your own time (beforehand) so that you will know more about what is going on during the rounds and discussions. In all honesty, I can't say I've always done that myself, but of the times I did that, I found it enhanced my learning and I could understand discussions better.

- Usually you could ask the house officers/medical officers which patient cases are useful for learning. In the clinic, with the doctor's permission, sometimes you can ask to read the case notes before patients are called in. This will help you ask more intelligent (relevant) questions, generate interesting clinical discussion and can enhance your learning.

- I think it is worth offering to help with things even though the answer is likely to be 'no, thank you'. There is always something to do — hand the gloves, pull the curtains, grab the case notes, open up the computer system, etc.

- However, it is important to understand that this is a tricky balance between being helpful and becoming obstructive. Hence, always ask and offer, but don't get discouraged if you get shot down. Most of us appreciate the offer as it is.

- Students who leave an impression are the ones who are keen and get involved. When I was doing General Surgery, there was an elective student who was always present for rounds and tagged on during on-calls, knew about the patients, helped with things, e.g. adjusting the light in the operation theatre, pulling curtains, helping with some simple house officer jobs. We found ourselves keen to tell her about any interesting patients/procedures. In addition, before the end of her electives, she already had an invitation to join the department.

- There are options to do electives locally and/or abroad. Both confer certain advantages. If you have the means, I would suggest you do a mixture of both. However, you need to be clear about your objectives before you set out to do your electives — whether it is to gain insight into the specialty to help you make that career choice, or to observe clinical practice in a different country and experience different cultures.

- If you have the means to do your electives overseas, sometimes it can be worthwhile doing it in a renowned unit as it could often offer you exposure and experience that can be inspiring. In addition, it will look good on your CV as owing to the competitive entry (even for electives) to these prestigious units.

- There are various strategies at play. Some students I know use their electives to rotate through all the local departments of the same specialty to enhance their presence in the specialty, some use them to do research, and so on.

- Basically, anything goes, as long as you have a clear idea of what you want to achieve during your electives.

7) Courses

- Having relevant courses on your CV reflects favourably because it shows that you are interested in the specialty and have made effort to deepen your clinical understanding and skills.

- This heading can be placed further back in your CV (after research, presentations, etc.) because courses mainly showcase interest and intent, less so effort (essentially anyone can get a course on their CV as long as they are willing to pay for it).

- There are generic courses and specialty-specific courses.
  - Generic courses, e.g. Basic Cardiac Life Support, Advanced Life Support, Basic Surgical Skills, Advanced Trauma Life Support
  - Specialty specific courses, e.g. Instructional Course in Microsurgery, Introductory Course in Interventional Cardiology, Basic Surgical Skills Course

- Your best bet is to ask your seniors (those who are in the specialty) as to which are relevant and adequate for your level.

- For those of you who are interested in surgical specialties, some of these courses provide hands-on opportunities (which can be rare at a junior level). This gives you the chance to make an honest assessment of your surgical dexterity to see if you are suited for the career.

8) Key skills

- As alluded to earlier, there are various skills which you can insert into your CV to showcase your clinical experience and capability. Some are generic skills, e.g. language and computer skills, some relate more to the specialty.

- To develop these items in your CV, you first need to know which skills are valued by the specialty. Again, this is something that you could find out from your seniors/current Residents. For instance, being able to insert chest drain may be a good demonstration of your manual dexterity and hence maybe beneficial for interventional cardiology/radiology. Ability to insert central line or arterial line is likely to be valued in General Surgery and Internal Medicine.

- Once you have an idea of what skills you need to acquire, you can actively seek out the opportunities to learn them. E.g. ask for Respiratory Medicine attachment when you are doing your Internal Medicine rotation so that you can get the chance to insert chest drains. It is helpful to do some pre-reading on the procedure so that you understand the basics (indication, the procedure itself and complications). You can also actively let the seniors know that you are really keen to try your hand at the procedure.

- Being able to utilise certain computer programs, e.g. SPSS, shows that you have dabbled in research work and can come in handy if you are planning to apply for the clinician-scientist track. There are courses organised by research units in most hospitals that teach SPSS.

- Language skills: I think this is the most understated skill of all, especially given our line of work. In this multiracial setting, nothing builds instant rapport with the patient like the ability to speak their language. It allows better understanding of the patient's concerns and can facilitate discussion with them. This thereby enables patient participation and management of their care.

- In addition to practical purposes, being able to speak multiple languages can be impressive. I remembered being awed by one TTSH ED Malay nurse's ability to converse in fluent Hokkien (better than mine) with an old patient who was trying to climb out of the trolley and by doing so succeeded in calming the patient down. Imagine being able to impart that sort of impression onto your bosses/selectors.

- It is worth picking up additional languages or dialects. Language courses are abundant. Hospitals like Tan Tock Seng Hospital organise dialect courses, e.g. Hokkien language for staff from time to time. I am not aware of whether they open these courses to medical students, but it may be worth enquiring.

9) **Teaching experience**

Why do it?

- It can showcase your diligence and commitment in being able to juggle teaching/leadership events amid your busy studies/clinical work.

- These skills are important in a career of medicine — it can be particularly helpful for patient education. In addition, as you progress in your career in medicine, you will be expected to take on the role of an educator in passing on knowledge/skills to your juniors.

- Not the least, it demonstrates other soft skills like organisation skills, time-management skills, ability to inspire, support and communicate with students, which can distinguish you from other candidates.

- You can learn through teaching. Teaching requires thorough understanding of the subject/concept before one can convey it in a comprehensible manner to the learners. Hence, through teaching, you develop a deeper and more persistent understanding of the topic.

- As anecdotal as it sounds, I found this to be true. As a house officer, I taught final-year medical students on 'testicular lump examination'. By the time I was running the fourth session of the same talk (for different rotations of students), I could literally do the whole talk without referring to the PowerPoint slides. I feel I could probably answer any question thrown at me on that subject at that time. This lasted till at least when I sat for my MRCS examinations a year later, which proved helpful.

- Teaching compels you to be creative and to think of different ways to explain the subject in order to facilitate understanding. It was certainly a great boost to my own presentation and facilitation skills.

- Most of all, I find myself learning how to be a 'student' through teaching. There is a certain amount of reciprocity in teaching. As I teach, I find myself responding differently to different students. Some students partake in the teaching session and respond in a way that encourages the tutor to share more. Introspectively, I noticed how I felt when working with these different students. This helped model my own learning behaviour. I learned to pick up the student behaviours that I felt were encouraging to me when I tutored them, and applied it as I continue to learn from my mentor.

- I am pretty sure that there have been many times where I have probably asked questions or behaved in a way that annoyed the hell out of my tutors. Hence, seeing how students react and the effect it has on me as a tutor helps me reflect and become a better student and learner.

How to do it?
- Teaching can be done on a formal or informal basis. Formal experience is usually better as it is likely that everyone else will have 'informal bedside teaching' within their repertoire.

- Watch out for teaching opportunities/events within medical school or in the clinical setting. Sign up to be a tutor/committee member and get involved.

- Seek out 'How to teach in medicine' or 'How to be a tutor' courses.

- If there isn't any teaching opportunity that you can find, create one. In my first house officer job, along with my colleague, we set up a 'Surgical Teaching for Finals' preparatory course for final-year students. We spotted the niche when we found a lack of teaching for surgical topics like hernia examination, testicular lump examination and vascular examination at the department. We then wrote a proposal to the Head of Department of Surgery, prepared teaching slides, taught the students on our own lunch breaks, got great feedback, enjoyed ourselves thoroughly and got an extra line in our CVs.

- Lastly, teaching does not necessarily have to be done in a clinical setting. You can also be doing teaching as part of your voluntary work.

10) Extra-curricular activities

- There are various extracurricular activities you can get involved in. For instance:

    o Voluntary work, e.g. SMILE project, nursing home work, animal rescue
    o Student boards/societies/interest groups
    o Organising committees for various events
    o Community activities
    o Sports and games

- Extracurricular activities give you organisational experience and the chance to work in a team. They also help you acquire various skills which can come in handy in your career in medicine, e.g. communication skills, leadership skills, social skills, time management, and the ability to prioritise.

- Quality of activities is often more important than quantity. If you are able to demonstrate the perseverance, continuity and depth in your involvement in the activities, it is often more impressive than just being involved on a superficial front.

- Sometimes having diverse interests can also be a conversation opener during interviews and may help your interviewer remember you.

11) Referees

- Getting a referee is not as simple as making that awkward request to a Consultant or Registrar who can barely remember who you are.

- In an ideal setting, one should get someone with whom you have developed close interactions and working relationships through rotations or clinical work.

- These are the people who will vouch for your credibility and provide an account of your strengths, character, skills and experience.

- Ideally, they should be consultants from the Specialty that you are applying into.

- Appreciably, for students, this can be difficult. Hence, lecturers or tutors whom you have worked with would be ideal. In addition, if you have a research project supervisor, they can come in as a referee too.

- It is good etiquette to seek your potential referees' permission before listing them as your referees.

- Singapore is a small community. The unsaid and unwritten truth is that word of mouth has more far-reaching impact than you could ever imagine. Hence, try and make an effort in choosing your referee and be polite when asking someone to be your referee.

How to Design Your CV

This section below is about how to present your CV in a neat and accessible manner in order to make it easy on the eye for your selectors/interviewer.

- Contents page — Have a contents page if your CV is very lengthy. It makes it appear more structured and makes it more accessible (easy to find the specific items)
- Number the pages
- The order of your heading should help highlight your achievements (e.g. put prizes/publications in the first few pages rather than the last)
- Clear headings — Having clear headings makes it easy for your interviewer to navigate
- Highlight — Bold or underlie certain items as appropriate
- Use separators — These can be lines, bolded words, or columns to help separate each section in your CV. These are helpful in dividing your CV into sections which are easily identified at a glance by your interviewers.
- Be neat — Have a consistent font, spacing and layout
- Be concise and relevant
- Length — Put in everything you need but keep it relevant
- Creative/artistic flair — I think being conservatively creative is perhaps the best I can suggest. I think there is nothing against adding a creative touch or graphics to your CV. However, the flamboyance should not be too excessive to take away your interviewers' attention from the contents of your CV.
- Get someone senior to look through your CV layout and give their advice — this is always helpful.
- Alternatively, you can ask to look at others' CVs and try and emulate the good points.

In Summary

I hope this chapter has been helpful. To conclude, CV preparation takes time. Please do not underestimate the length of time needed to achieve items in your CV before your application/interview. Courses and examination happen only on certain dates. Research takes time to complete and mature into presentations or publications. So do get started as soon as possible.

Reference

1. Membership of the Royal Colleges of Physicians of the United Kingdom. Choosing the right time to take your MRCP (UK) Examinations. MRCPUK 2018. Available from URL: https://www.mrcpuk.org/mrcpuk-examinations/advice-guidance-and-preparation/choosing-right-time-take-your-mrcpuk. [Accessed 23/12/18].

4

Research and Publications

"If we knew what it was we were doing, it would not be called research, would it?" — Albert Einstein

Key Points

- For purposes of Residency application, research and publication demonstrates your interest in the field, allows rapport building and increases your visibility within the department.
- The general flow of research process involves formulating research idea, doing a literature search, designing your study, developing a research protocol, ethics application, data collection, analysis, write up and submission for publication.
- It is worth doing a research protocol at the beginning of your project because it forces you to systematically think about every single aspect of your study. This can help you decide on the feasibility and viability of your study.

- Research protocol also provides you or your team members a framework to refer to during your study and can be used in your final write up.
- For your first few projects — choose the right mentor. Choose a mentor who has the experience in research and publications and more importantly has the time to guide you in the research process.

Why is Research Important?

Medical research is fundamental in advancing healthcare. It plays a pivotal role in providing us with evidence to guide our daily practice, giving us the ability to apply a scientific approach to our day-to-day clinical decisions.

At present, there is more emphasis than ever on the need to develop research skills. Even if you have no intention in pursuing an academic career, performing research has its relevance in our day-to-day clinical practice. By immersing oneself in the research process, medical students/junior doctors will able to train themselves to understand evidence within the literature, extract relevant information, perform critical analysis, and apply this evidence in clinical decisions.

Moreover, for the purposes of application into the Residency system, research and publication is a way of demonstrating your interest in the field. It shows effort on your part. Doing research for a department also increases your visibility within the department. It allows consultants and work colleagues to see your work ethic, drive, communication and organisational skills. Overall, having research and publications under your belt is likely to increase your competitiveness in the application for Residency.

Beyond Residency, as a consultant, research is a way of improving your practice, establishing yourself in your field of interest and improving patient care.

Why is Research Difficult?

Time consuming — Research is time consuming. It takes time to plan, to do literature search, to do the ethics application, to collect data, to write up, so on and so forth. The main constraint lies where there is often no time set aside for you to do research. In other words, research is often done in our own time. That means research will be competing against your other commitments such as passing the MBBS or doing your clinical work (on-calls, clinic duties, OT, preparing morbidity and mortality, preparing for journal club, etc.). It is completely reasonable and necessary that one prioritises the MBBS/clinical work over research. They are your main responsibilities as a student/doctor. Hence, research often gets put on the back burner. In addition, things don't always go as planned. Various roadblocks exist on the path of research. The research process may be impeded by various delays such as fulfilling the multiple arduous requirements for ethics application, problems with participant recruitment, issues with funding or equipment and other logistic problems. It takes a lot of dedication and academic rigour to perform and complete a research project.

No clear overview of research process — If you are trying to do research for the very first time, it can be difficult as most of us will not have much idea of what the research process entails. The question often asked is — how and where do I get started? Furthermore, there will always be obstacles within the research process. These can come in the form of problems in obtaining ethics approval, dealing with missing data, unexpected findings, adverse events, and so on. For a first-timer, it can be difficult to navigate through these obstacles. Often they become hindrances that prevent students/junior doctors from completing a research project. This is where an experienced and dedicated mentor/supervisor comes in handy as they can guide you in resolving those issues.

Unfamiliarity with the field — As medical students or junior doctors, we lack periphery knowledge. This periphery knowledge is crucial in deciphering what research topic is feasible and publishable. It takes this sort of clinical knowledge to be aware of what topics have been extensively researched, which topics are the focus of grant calls, which are of good utility and which have the potential to be published. Unfortunately, this is the sort of knowledge that comes along only after immersing oneself in the specialty long enough (familiarity with clinical work, attending enough conferences, awareness of latest research evidence). Again, this is why it is useful to have an experienced and dedicated supervisor who can guide you through these aspects.

Statistics! — I don't know about you. I basically slept through my statistics classes in university and I sure as hell regret it now. It can be very painful to be at near completion of a research project and realising that you have an inadequate sample size or that you have not collected the necessary data to answer your clinical question. Had you been aware of the statistic calculations necessary, you would have ensured power calculation was done. Personally I have been heavily reliant on statisticians (bless them!). However, I have just booked myself into a biostatistics course to gain more understanding. I think you should too! Alternatively, pay attention in your statistics class!

Having stumbled multiple times in my own journey in research and publication (with five to six projects which amounted to nothing after hours of blood and sweat), below are some tips and general information that I hope will be helpful to you.

General Flow of Research

Below is a general flow of a research process.

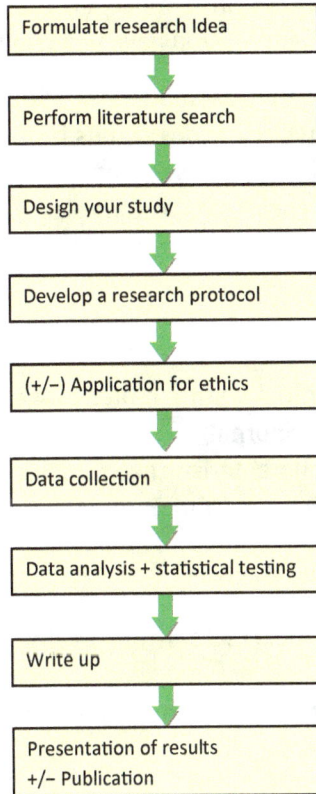

```
┌─────────────────────────────────┐
│ Formulate research Idea         │
└─────────────────────────────────┘
              ↓
┌─────────────────────────────────┐
│ Perform literature search       │
└─────────────────────────────────┘
              ↓
┌─────────────────────────────────┐
│ Design your study               │
└─────────────────────────────────┘
              ↓
┌─────────────────────────────────┐
│ Develop a research protocol     │
└─────────────────────────────────┘
              ↓
┌─────────────────────────────────┐
│ (+/−) Application for ethics    │
└─────────────────────────────────┘
              ↓
┌─────────────────────────────────┐
│ Data collection                 │
└─────────────────────────────────┘
              ↓
┌─────────────────────────────────┐
│ Data analysis + statistical testing │
└─────────────────────────────────┘
              ↓
┌─────────────────────────────────┐
│ Write up                        │
└─────────────────────────────────┘
              ↓
┌─────────────────────────────────┐
│ Presentation of results         │
│ +/− Publication                 │
└─────────────────────────────────┘
```

1. Formulate research idea

Developing a research question can be challenging. As a student/ junior doctor, most of my research ideas came from Consultants. More often than not, you will be 'arrowed' to do certain projects by Consultants in the department. If not, you could always make yourself (readily) available by letting the Consultants know that you are keen to do projects during your attachment and rotation with them. This is often helpful as Consultants might not always have research projects ready at hand at the time when you ask, but should one arise, you could be the first in line to know. Word of advice though, elective attachments or clinical rotations often fly by and before you know it, the stint will be over. Hence, it is best to pre-plan and get in touch with the Consultants in advance, in order to capitalise on the time and location advantage you have when in the department.

Alternatively, the (true) traditional way of getting a research idea or formulating research questions comes from unanswered clinical issues. Should there be any clinical questions arising from your day-to-day clinical work, these can be formulated into research questions. Typically research ideas concern (but are not limited to):

a) **Diagnosis**

- What are the most common presenting symptoms in nasopharyngeal carcinoma?
- What are the characteristic examination findings of patients with Klippel–Feil syndrome?

b) **Aetiology and Risk Factors**

- What are the risk factors for developing nasopharyngeal cancer?
- Does increased body mass index lead to more severe obstructive sleep apnea?

c) **Investigations**

- How does drug-induced sleep nasoendoscopy compare to computed tomography in the evaluation of sleep apnea?
- Is a raised lymphocyte count a predictor of infectious mononucleosis in patients who present with tonsillitis?

d) **Treatment**

- How does septoplasty influence olfactory function?
- How does surgery compare to treatment chemoradiotherapy in the treatment of condition B?
- What is the current practice in treatment of otitis media?

e) Prognosis

- What are the chances of recovery for patients who present with post-traumatic anosmia?
- What are the long-term risks of developing cardiovascular complications in patients with mild, moderate or severe obstructive sleep apnea?
- Do recurrent ear infections lead to deafness?

f) Quality of Life Study

- What is the quality of life of allergic rhinitis sufferers?
- How does quality of life differ between patients who underwent surgery or chemoradiotherapy for laryngeal cancer?

g) Others

Research in medical training/teaching, development of animal models, development of simulation machine for training, study of cost-effectiveness of an investigation or treatment.

Try and heighten your awareness of all the clinical questions lying around. Try and spot the knowledge gap within current practices. Often a lot of these questions get flagged during departmental audit meetings, mortality and morbidity meetings or journal clubs. Many of these are great and viable research ideas.

Once you have the research idea, next comes formulation of the research question itself. The **PICO** format (Sackett *et al.*, 1997) represents a simple yet systematic framework for one to (think through) and develop the research question:

- **P (Population):** Population/patient or problem of interest
- **I (Intervention):** Investigation, treatment, exposure to certain risk factors
- **C (Control):** Comparison to control/healthy population/ placebo/standard treatment
- **O (Outcome):** Outcome of interest

So for instance, to formulate the clinical question 'How does septoplasty influence olfactory function?' into the PICO format:

- P (Population): Patients who require septoplasty
- I (Intervention): Septoplasty
- C (Control): Healthy controls who did not undergo septoplasty
- O (Outcome): Olfactory function

Another example: 'Does recurrent otitis media lead to deafness in children?'

- P (Population): Children
- I (Intervention): Exposure to recurrent otitis media
- C (Control): Children without recurrent otitis media
- O (Outcome): Deafness

After the research question is formulated, it is important to consider the practicality of your research question. As proposed by Hulley *et al.* (Hulley *et al.*, 2007), the **FINER** criteria is good list to think through when formulating one's research question.

- **F (Feasibility):** This is one of the most important considerations. Is there a sufficient patient/population? Does the research require funding? Where and how will you obtain the list of patients for the study, e.g. via theatre records? Do you have sufficient time to carry out the research (e.g. if a research project involves recruitment of patients over a two-year period, it might be difficult for you as a student/junior doctor to follow through).

- **I (Interesting):** This is not absolute, but the research topic should be something of interest to you and to your community. This makes it more publishable.

- **N (Novel):** It would be advantageous that your research idea adds something new to the existing literature. However, it could also be an extension to previous findings.

- **E (Ethical):** All research that involves any patients, patient records, human subjects, studying of tissue, animals, study of investigation/treatment/intervention requires ethics approval. More information can be obtained from: https://www.research.nhg.com.sg/wps/wcm/connect/romp/nhgromp/hspp/dssrbfaq

- **R (Relevant):** The more I delve and dabble with research, the more important it becomes that I ask the 'so what?' question. In other words, what is the relevance of your research to clinical practice? How does it influence or change things? Again, you will find that this is not always absolute. However, doing research which has relevance/potential impact gives meaning to your work and can help motivate you through crappy research days when hurdles are plenty and things don't go well.

2.   Performing literature search

Literature search is a systematic and comprehensive search for materials on a topic from various databases. Performing a literature search prior to embarking on a research project is important for a few reasons

- It helps you know what data/information is available in the current literature and whether your idea is novel.

- If your idea is not novel, you could see how you could add on to the existing literature — e.g. expansion of data, adding a different perspective.

- You can take reference of the study design of the existing studies.

- Literature search allows you to have an estimate of the potential sample size required.

- Literature search is also useful in providing an academic basis for your research in the write-up of your research protocol.

The process generally involves:

a) **Defining your research question**
b) **Identifying key words**
c) **Searching databases**
d) **Selecting abstracts and obtaining the full articles**
e) **Evaluating and recording your findings**

a) **Defining your research question**

Decide on what you are interested in finding out and formulate the question, e.g. 'What are the effects of passive smoking on children with otitis media with effusion?'

b) **Identify key words**

- Key words in the question above include 'passive smoking', 'children', 'otitis media'

- Remember to broaden your list of key words with synonyms
  o 'passive smoking', 'nicotine', 'cigarette smoking'
  o 'otitis media with effusion', 'middle ear effusion', 'glue ear'
  o 'children', 'child', 'infant', 'toddler', 'paediatric'

- Add the acronyms, e.g. otitis media with effusion = 'OME'

- Remember the different spellings, e.g. 'pediatric' versus 'paediatric' (add them all to broaden your search).

c) **Searching databases**

- There are various databases available. Just to name a few: PUBMED, EMBASE, COCHRANE LIBRARY. I sometimes use Google Scholar as well, which can give pretty good yield and occasionally throws in the full article as well.

- Combine your keywords with Boolean operators (**AND, OR** or **NOT**) to perform your search.

- For instance: (passive smoking OR nicotine OR cigarette smoking) AND (otitis media with effusion OR middle ear effusion OR glue ear OR OME) AND (children OR child OR pediatric).

- Example of search results as below:

d) **Selecting abstracts and obtaining full articles**

- From the search results as above, you can then click on the links and look at the abstract (as shown below) and determine its relevance to your question.

- If you deem it relevant or if you are not fully sure, you may want to obtain the full article to browse through.

- Full articles come in the form of hard copy (kept in libraries) or soft copy (online).

- In this Internet age, I get most of my full articles online unless hard copies are the only available ones.

- Most universities and hospitals have access to a variable number of journals. They can be accessed via accounts made available to university students, and some are readily available on hospital intranets. If you are not sure where to find them, best bet is usually to enquire via your hospital or university librarian.

- The NUS library has very comprehensive list of journals which can be accessed (with an account + password) via: https://libportal.nus.edu.sg/frontend/ejournals-home

- Generally, you will first have to look for the journal, and then search the journal index according to the year or volume/issue of publication in order to locate your article.

- So for instance, the article below was published in *Int J Pediatr Otorhinolaryngol* in 2010, volume 74 issue 6.

Ξ NCBI   Resources ☑   How To ☑

Pub**Med**.gov   PubMed   ▼
US National Library of Medicine
National Institutes of Health   Advanced

Display Settings: ☑ Abstract   Send to: ☑

Int J Pediatr Otorhinolaryngol. 2010 Jun;74(6):677-83. doi: 10.1016/j.ijporl.2010.03.023. Epub 2010 Apr 22.

Risk factors for otitis media among preschool, rural Indian children.

Sophia A[1], Isaac R, Rebekah G, Brahmadathan K, Rupa V.

⊕ Author information

Abstract

OBJECTIVE: To establish the role of various risk factors for otitis media among preschool, rural Indian children.

METHODS: A cross sectional study of 800 children was undertaken to determine the prevalence of otitis media. Thereafter, using a case control study design, all the cases and an equal number of controls were compared in terms of various common risk factors for otitis media. The 13 risk factors studied were age, sex, socioeconomic status (SES), nutritional status, balwadi attendance, duration of breast feeding, passive smoking, exposure to household smoke, persistent rhinorrhoea, positive throat culture, snoring, seasonal rhinitis and allergic rhinitis. Bivariate association between these risk factors and otitis media was studied using chi-square test of proportions. Multivariate logistic regression analysis was done by including the variables which were significant at $p=0.35$ in the bivariate analysis.

RESULTS: From the cross sectional study, the prevalence of otitis media was found to be 8.6%, roughly half the prevalence obtained 10 years previously from the same region. Otitis media with effusion (OME) was the commonest manifestation of otitis media (6%) with 3.8% having bilateral disease. Ear wax was seen in 27.5% of subjects. Eighteen (2.3%) children failed the screening audiometry test set at 40 dB HL. Sociodemographic factors among cases and controls were comparable. The prime risk factors for otitis media identified by bivariate analysis included persistent rhinorrhoea, snoring and seasonal rhinitis. On multivariate logistic regression analysis, persistent rhinorrhoea ($p<0.01$, O.R.=7.56, 95%C.I. 2.73 - 20.92), snoring ($p=0.01$, O.R.=4.89, 95% C.I.1.32 - 18.17), seasonal rhinitis($p=0.02$, OR=5.93,95% CI=1.33-26.51) and passive smoking ($p=0.04$, O.R.=3.29, 95%C.I. 1.05-10.33) were found to be important risk factors for otitis media. Age, sex, SES, parental education, seasonal or allergic rhinitis, inadequate breast feeding and exposure to household smoke were not significant risk factors.

CONCLUSIONS: Otitis media continues to have a high prevalence among South Indian children. Persistent rhinorrhoea, snoring, seasonal rhinitis and passive smoking are the chief risk factors for the disease. Measures to reduce the prevalence of otitis media by addressing these risk factors are urgently required.

- Using NUS library as an example, first ensure you have selected the 'e-journal' tab. Type in the journal name: 'Int J Pediatr Otorhinolaryngol', as shown below:

- Press enter or click on the arrow and you will get the screen below.

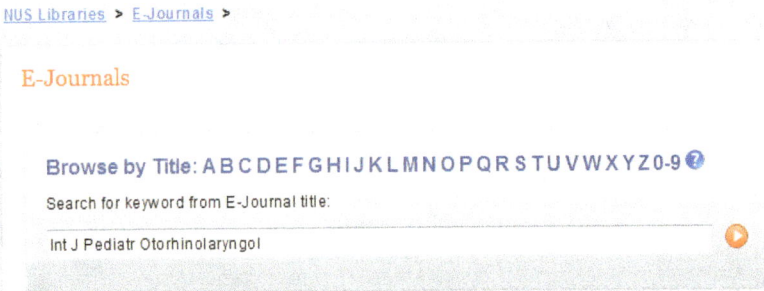

NUS Libraries > E-Journals >

E-Journals

Browse by Title: A B C D E F G H I J K L M N O P Q R S T U V W X Y Z 0-9

Search for keyword from E-Journal title:

Int J Pediatr Otorhinolaryngol

To add/remove titles to My Favourites, please log in and add the E-Journals widget.

Title	Publisher	Coverage	Add/Remove	Codes
International journal of pediatric otorhinolaryngology		v1:n1 (01 Jul 1979)		
International journal of pediatric otorhinolaryngology extra		v1:n1 (01 Mar 2006)		

- Click on the journal title and it will require you to enter your account and password; it will then bring you to the journal website

- Go to the right corner and search for the year/ volume/issue that you are looking for, in this instance: 2010, volume 74 issue 6

- Click on the volume and scroll down to the page to search for your article

Head and neck manifestation and prognosis of Langerhans' cell histiocytosis in children Original Research Article
Pages 669-673
R. Nicollas, A. Rome, H. Belaich, S. Roman, M. Volk, J.C. Gentet, G. Michel, J.M. Triglia
▸ Abstract   PDF (212 K)

The effect of gastric decompression on postoperative nausea and emesis in pediatric, tonsillectomy patients Original Research Article
Pages 674-676
O. Chukudebelu, D.S. Leonard, A. Healy, D. McCoy, D. Charles, S. Hone, M. Rafferty
PDF (85 K)

Risk factors for otitis media among preschool, rural Indian children Original Research Article
Pages 677-683
A. Sophia, Rita Isaac, Grace Rebekah, K. Brahmadathan, V. Rupa
▸ Abstract   PDF (205 K)

Impact of oseltamivir treatment on the incidence and course of acute otitis media in children with influenza Original Research Article
Pages 684-688
Birgit Winther, Stan L. Block, Keith Reisinger, Regina Dutkowski
▸ Abstract   PDF (150 K)

Nasal nitric oxide in children with adenoidal hypertrophy: A preliminary study Original Research Article
Pages 689-693

- Click on the 'pdf' link under your article and that will give you your full article
- Remember to save a copy of the pdf of your article or copy down the link

Contents lists available at ScienceDirect

International Journal of Pediatric Otorhinolaryngology

Journal homepage: www.elsevier.com/locate/ijporl

ELSEVIER

Risk factors for otitis media among preschool, rural Indian children

A. Sophia [a], Rita Isaac [b], Grace Rebekah [c], K. Brahmadathan [d], V. Rupa [a,*]

[a] Department of ENT, Christian Medical College, Vellore, India
[b] Department of Community Health, Christian Medical College, Vellore, India
[c] Department of Biostatistics, Christian Medical College, Vellore, India
[d] Department of Microbiology, Christian Medical College, Vellore, India

ARTICLE INFO

Article history:
Received 17 January 2010
Received in revised form 7 March 2010
Accepted 8 March 2010
Available online 22 April 2010

ABSTRACT

Objective: To establish the role of various risk factors for otitis media among preschool, rural Indian children.
Methods: A cross sectional study of 800 children was undertaken to determine the prevalence of otitis media. Thereafter, using a case control study design, all the cases and an equal number of controls were compared in terms of various common risk factors for otitis media. The 13 risk factors studied were age,

d) Evaluating and recording your search findings

- You can do this systematically by creating tables — recording the authors, year, study design, outcome measures, significant results, and make some comments on the article (shown below in Figure 4.1).

Author	Design	Follow Up	N	Inclusion Criteria	Outcome Measures	Outcome
Khosla 2012	Meta-analysis		N = 1148	FESS patients	Blood loss	Preoperative steroid more beneficial than placebo (less blood loss 28 ml). Statistically significant
Sieskiewicz A 2006	RCT		N = 36. −18 with 30 mg pred 5D −18 control	Severe nasal polyposis	Total blood loss. Visualisation surgical field.	Blood loss slightly better in pred group ($p = 0.66$). Visualisation better in pred group ($p = 0.03$)
Wright 2007	Double blind RCT	2 wk 1 mth 3 mth 6 mth	N = 26 −13 pred 30 mg 5D **preop** and 9D postop −13 placebo	Nasal polypo- sis	Intraop findings. Postop symptom. Endoscopic findings	Intraop–surgery easier in pred gp, no diff in blood loss/op time Post op. symptoms

Figure 4.1   Summary of papers on "Primary FESS for nasal polyposis."

3. Designing your study

The study design is important in determining the reliability of the study's conclusions and its scientific quality. Selection of a suitable study design is important in reducing potential bias and confounding factors. In practical terms, selecting a study design is often a compromise between producing research of high scientific quality and constraints on time and resources.

At times, the study design used is also a consideration of what is feasible and sensible. As it is very aptly summarised by the article 'Parachute use to prevent death and major trauma related to gravitational challenge: systematic review of randomised controlled trials', published in *BMJ* in 2003 (available from: http://www.bmj.com/content/327/7429/1459) — it is impossible to perform a randomised controlled trial to evaluate the efficacy of parachute use in preventing the risk of injury following a free fall. (Highly recommended read! This is an ingenious piece of satire, disparaging and lamenting our sometimes over-obsession with evidence-based medicine.)

There are different levels of evidence. Below is the hierarchy of evidence from the National Guideline Clearinghouse, US Department of Health & Human Services:

IA   Evidence from meta-analysis of randomized controlled trials

IB   Evidence from at least one randomized controlled trial

IIA Evidence from at least one controlled study without randomisation

IIB Evidence from at least one other type of quasi-experimental study

III Evidence from non-experimental descriptive studies, such as comparative studies, correlation studies, and case-control studies

IV   Evidence from expert committee reports or opinions or clinical experience of respected authorities, or both

Study designs can be broadly divided into **Experimental** and **Observation studies**. **Experimental study** involves the evaluation of the effect of a treatment of intervention on the recruited population. It can be divided into:

- **Randomised controlled trial**
  - Randomised controlled trials can be divided into Double-blinded, Single-blinded or Non-blinded trials.

  - The random assignment of study subjects into two groups (study and control group) equalises their baseline characteristics thereby providing the strongest evidence for any causal link demonstrated by the results. This is important as it ensures that in the long run, the study group and control group will be balanced in terms of known and unknown prognostic factors (which could have affected the outcomes).

  - The blinding process removes bias from investigators and removes any factor that can affect the evaluation process.

  - A double-blind design is one in which neither the study subject or evaluator/investigator knows the intervention of which the subject was assigned.

  - Single blind is where either the study subject or evaluator is blinded. It is not always possible to blind the subjects, e.g. if you are evaluating the effect of counselling session on patient outcome. But in this instance, you can still blind the evaluator.

- **Non-randomised trial (quasi-experimental study)**
  - A quasi-experimental study is one in which treatment allocation is not random. It allows the researcher to control the assignment into study or control group, often on the basis of some criteria. It is used when randomisation is impractical or unethical.

o Some describe this as a 'natural experiment', as it is often a study of certain subpopulations for which the characteristics are determined by nature or simply not within the control of the researcher.

o Pros: It is easier to implement compared with randomised controlled trials. As it is a 'natural experiment', it allows generalisation and application of the result findings to population with similar characteristics as those in the study group.

o Cons: The lack of randomisation pre-disposes the study to confounders that can affect the outcome.

Observational studies involve monitoring the outcome of study subjects (without providing intervention/treatment).

- **Cohort study**
  o A cohort study is one in which a group of people with certain attributes/characteristics/exposure to risk factors are followed up to determine the incidence of a disease or an outcome.

  o Can be divided in to Prospective or Retrospective cohort study.

  o For instance — one can study the impact of appendicitis (characteristics of a group of patients) and the development of adhesion colic (outcome).

  o Pros: This study design is suitable for study of rare diseases, or study of unusual association. It is useful in examining the development of disease/condition after a rare/highly specific exposure. Moreover, it allows absolute measurement of risk of developing a condition/disease.

  o Cons:
    ▪ The cohort is selected by the investigator, therefore being prone to bias. In addition, there are no controls

to compare outcomes — it is therefore difficult to justify and quantify the outcome that is observed.

- In addition, cohorts can sometimes be difficult to identify. For instance, if you are trying to investigate the impact of a contaminated batch of paracetamol on pregnant women — paracetamol is a non-tracked drug, and its sales during any given period will be huge because it is a common drug. So it would be a huge (near impossible) undertaking to track down all those who have bought and consumed the drug, let alone those who are pregnant AND consumed the drug at THAT period where it was contaminated.

- **Case-control study**
  - A case-control study is one in which two groups with different outcomes/diseases are compared to look for possible causal attributes.

  - Control is a standard for comparison of effects or variability.

  - For instance — one can examine patients with nasopharyngeal carcinoma (study group) and those without (control group) and examine their exposure to salted fish in their diet.

  - Pros: It is relatively easy to carry out. It can provide preliminary information on rare diseases or condition where there is little information available regarding the association between the risk factor and the condition. In addition, study groups are usually ease to define specifically (e.g. researchers can identify patients with certain diseases and recruit them into the study).

  - Cons: In case-controlled studies, the study population (with certain risk factors) is often recruited for observation of outcome. It is often difficult to obtain accurate information about their exposure status to the risk factor, as this is done retrospectively. In addition, it is not randomised, hence results can be affected by confounding factors.

4. Developing a research protocol

A research protocol is a document in which you detail every aspect of your study. There are various formats for research protocol. Typically a research protocol will require you to fill in details of the study, including background, current evidence, objectives, outcome measures, hypothesis, study design, rationale for choice of design, patient recruitment methods, inclusion and exclusion criteria, sample size calculation, intervention (drug/devices), data analysis and statistics, consent process, data handling and confidentiality issues, potential risks and benefits, incident reporting and so on.

Why Bother?

A research protocol should be done at the beginning of a research project rather than only when needed (e.g. ethics application). This is because

- It forces you to critically and systematically think about every single aspect of your study — feasibility, whether your design is adequate to answer your research questions, the time required to recruit enough participants and so on. These are important factors which help decide whether your research project is a no-go, or if it is something that is achievable. Again, this is much better done at the beginning rather than realising painfully in the midst of the project (after hours of blood and sweat) that you might not have a large enough sample size to reach any conclusion.

- It provides you or your team members a framework/guide to refer to in the midst of your study.
- If you are working in big teams, the research protocol acts as a standard operation manual.

- It can be used repeatedly for various applications — ethics application, funding or grant applications.
- It can also provide a backbone for your final write-up.

There are various formats of research protocol you could utilise. However, just a tip, it is best to use the research protocol template required for ethics application. Quite often, it is comprehensive enough and more likely than not, most of our research requires ethics approval. The template that I tend to stick to is the 'Study Protocol Template' from NHG DSRB (type in 'study protocol template dsrb' in Google, and you will find it).

The general headings required within a study protocol include:

— study title
— protocol version and date
— investigator names and designations
— study site(s)
— study background and rationale, hypothesis
— study population
— study design
— study schedule
— trial products (if any) or treatment proposed (if any)
— data analysis
— statistical methods and power calculation
— data and patient safety

When starting off, it could be easier if you have an existing (someone else's) study protocol for reference. In addition, following completion, it is best you review and discuss the study protocol with your supervisor.

5. **Ethics application**
    - Ethics in research is a safeguard to help protect the welfare and rights of research participants.
    - What type of study requires ethics approval?

In essence, any research, testing, evaluation involving patients, staff, premises or facilities of the institution will require ethics approval. This includes:

- o Questionnaires
- o Administering intervention (drugs, vaccines, surgery, radiation)
- o Use of human tissue
- o Experimentation involving human/animals

- Ethics application can be done via the ethics committee in each institution

  - o National Healthcare Group Domain Specific Review Board (NHG DSRB) — https://www.research.nhg.com.sg/sop/process/ROMP/Admin_Intranet_Login

  - o SingHealth Centralised Institutional Review Board — https://ishare.singhealth.com.sg/

  - o National University of Singapore Institutional Review Board (NUS IRB) — http://www.nus.sg/irb/

- First tip about ethics applications — if you think you need one, get started early. This takes time. To their credit, the ethics committees do meet quite frequently (as frequest as every month).

- However, there are a few things which might cause a delay

  - o After you click submit, your application still needs to go through approval by a 'Departmental Representative' (usually a head of department or designated consultant) and an 'Institutional Representative', before DSRB reviews your application.

  - o Depending on the completeness of your application and complexity of your study, there may be multiple exchanges of queries, replies and amendments.

- Exemptions

There are some studies that can be exempted from DSRB (however, you still have to put in an application to ask for an exemption). These include (but are not limited to):

  o Review of normal clinical practice, e.g. collection of existing data (without any deviation from standard practice), audit of surgeon's surgical outcomes
  o Normal educational practices, e.g. evaluating teaching techniques
  o Review of public programs, e.g. review of efficacy of public talks
  o Case reports (provided the patient has consented and confidentiality is maintained)
  o If you are not sure whether your study qualifies for exemption, it is best to enquire with the respective Institutional Review Boards (IRB).

- Expedited review can be granted if the chairperson determines that your study involves minimal risk. Typically those that involve non-invasive procedures/no procedures qualify for expedited review.

- Basic documents required include:

  o DSRB application form
  o Study Protocol (use the template provided by the DSRB/ institution)
  o Curriculum vitae, CITI certification and financial disclosure of the principal Investigator, co-Investigators and other study members
  o Others (if relevant): consent documents, patient information sheet, questionnaires/survey tools, data collection forms, previous publications, grant documents, and so on.

- Basic requirement for investigators

The minimum training required depends on your participation role. For principal investigator and site principal investigators, Collaborative Institutional Training Initiative's (CITI) Programme certification and completion of Good Clinical Practice (GCP) course are required. For Co-investigators, CITI programme certification is required. For other study team members, neither GCP and CITI certification is not required. However, NHG requires all study members to complete the CITI Financial Conflicts of Interest Course.

Minimum training requirements for each institution are available on the websites below:

1) Singhealth: https://research.singhealth.com.sg/pages/centralisedinstitutionalreviewboard.aspx
2) NHG: https://www.research.nhg.com.sg/wps/wcm/connect/romp/nhgromp/o6+conducting+research/intro+min+training+requirements
3) NUHS: http://www.nus.edu.sg/irb/

For all three institutions, there is a minimum training required for principal investigators and co-investigators. This includes completion of the CITI program

- CITI program: https://www.citiprogram.org/

The CITI programme (Collaborative Institutional Training Initiative) is the initiative of the University of Miami that provides web-based research education materials. These online training courses are designed to improve our understanding of ethics principles involving human subject research, to be aware of potential risks and harm associated with biomedical research on human subjects, as well as understanding of the basic regulations in research conduct.

To enrol, you will have to create an account at the web-page provided above. There are several modules, each of which consists of reading material and a short quiz at the end. You will have to achieve an average score of 80% on all quizzes in order to pass. There is no negative marking. If you fail, you just need to retake it. It takes about 2 hours or so to complete. At the end of the training, you will be given a CITI e-certificate which you should download and safe-keep a copy. This is the same copy which you will have to upload to your IRB/DSRB account.

o Good Clinical Practice (GCP) Programme

This is available as both online and classroom formats. There are various institutions which offer this course at different time points. They include:

— NHG Research and Development Office
— Singhealth Investigational Medicine Unit and Singhealth Academy
— National University of Singapore

This course is a minimum training requirement for principal investigators and site principal investigators. It provides insight into good clinical conduct when performing research. Its modules include research ethics framework, informed consent, clinical trial safety, fraud and misconduct, what to organise, how to maintain an investigator file, and so on. Information regarding the dates, cost and programme of the course can be obtained from the research office of each institution.

For more information, look up:
https://www.singhealthacademy.edu.sg/Pages/Good-Clinical-Practice.aspx

https://www.research.nhg.com.sg/wps/wcm/connect/romp/
nhgromp/04+training+and+education/training+courses+
workshops/sg+gcp+course

6. **Data collection + data entry**

- Good data management makes analysis easier. It also makes it easier to extract information from your data for further studies and allows you to share your data with other investigators easily.

- There should be consistency in your data management to ensure good quality data. Data collectors should be briefed about a standard data collection procedure. For instance, in a study looking at complications following laparoscopic cholecystectomy, the research team may want to standardise the source of the data. It is therefore important to ensure all team members check for presence of complications from the diagnosis coding at the discharge summary, as well as to look through postoperative documentations to check for the presence of complications.

- There are a few good tools for data entry, which include Microsoft Excel and SPSS.

- In entering your data into Excel or SPSS, often on the X-axis you have your variables. There should be a data dictionary, usually in 'sheet 2' in Excel for you to explain what those variables mean and what are the symbols/numbers used to represent the categories. This makes it easier for the next person/other investigators to understand your data and makes it easy for communication.

- Example of sheet 1 (data collection)

	A	B	C	D	E	F	G
1	SN	Gender	Co-morb	BP1	BP2	BP3	
2	1	0	3	170	160	160	
3	2	0	2	180	160	150	
4	3	0	2	165	170	150	
5	4	1	1	190	180	150	
6	5	1	1	200	180	160	
7	6	0	3	170	150	140	
8	7	1	1	165	150	140	
9	8	0	3	188	180	170	
10	9	1	2	178	170	160	
11	10	0	1	150	140	140	

Sheet1   Sheet2   Sheet3

- Example of sheet 2 (data dictionary)

	A	B	C
1	Variable	Variable meaning	Categories
2	SN	Serial number	
3	Gender	Gender	Male = 0 Female =1
4	Co-morb	Number of co-morbidities	1 Commorbid = 1, 2 commorbid = 2, >2 commobids = 3
5	BP1	Baseline systolic blood pressure before intervention	
6	BP2	Systolic blood pressure 1 month post intervention	
7	BP3	Systolic blood pressure 3 month post intervention	

- If you could help it, it is best to enter the data straight into Excel to avoid extra work. Some researchers create a data collection form (e.g. Microsoft Word Document or Microsoft Acess), and then transfer them later on into Excel or SPSS.

- This is sometimes necessary for certain situations, such as for postal questionnaire survey.

- However, in terms fix of recording findings from medical case notes, I prefer to enter it straight into Excel/SPSS. I think the process of double data entry is prone to error (especially during data transfer) and time consuming.

- Main problems with data collection and entry are usually related to completeness and accuracy of data.

- If you are performing questionnaire surveys, try and make sure you check through your participants' questionnaire right after they complete it and whilst the participants are still around. This is so that you can get them to fill in any missing bits.

- When performing retrospective data collection (for instance, looking through medical records for information), it can be difficult to account for missing data.

- You may want to be creative in identifying all the data sources you need. For instance, apart from physical case notes, other sources of information include hospital computer systems, polyclinic records, confirming with patients/ participants during their clinic visit or via telephone. However, bear in mind all these methods should be detailed and submitted for ethics approval prior to carrying them out.

- There should be a record of any significant events that occur during the period of data collection. Examples of these events include unanticipated complications experienced by research subjects, subjects dropping out of study and their reasons, and so on. These events need to be reported to the Ethics committee.

- It is also important to have a record of these events, as it can help you understand anomalies and identify bias in your data.

- In terms of accuracy of data, it is important that the both the principal investigator and the person collecting data are clear about the objective of the study, what each strand of data means, and for them to be able to communicate with each other should any queries arise during data collection.

- So for instance, when performing a study to validate a questionnaire, the data collector may be tempted to explain to the subject when a question is raised about the question-naire. However, it is important that the person collecting data does not try to give the study subject an interpretation of what the question means. Rather, study subjects should be encourage to fill it in on their own based on their understanding of the questions.

- It is also useful to make a remark on any data which you are unsure of so that you can re-visit it with your supervisor/principal investigator later when possible.

- Always save your data as you are entering it (apparently the gold standard is to click on the save button every 30 minutes!) and always backup your data on a second thumb drive/computer.

7. **Data analysis + statistical testing**

- Again, Microsoft Excel and SPSS are good software for data analysis and statistical testing.

- For statistical testing, as mentioned previously, I am rather reliant on my friendly statistician. However, I do think it is useful to learn the basics so that you could at least communicate sensibly with your statistician.

- Most hospitals/universities have in-house statisticians. Phone the hospital switchboard for their contact information (ask for statistician or clinical research unit or investigational medicine unit).

- It is useful to be clear about what your objectives and hypotheses are when discussing with your statistician so that they can help apply correct statistical testing methods to assist in providing an answer to your research question.

- It is useful to have (similar) previously published papers at hand so that you can refer to what statistical test methods they used.

8. Write-up

So, you have jumped through all prior hoops of designing your own project, obtaining ethics approval, collecting data and analysis your data. You are now armed with the results from your study and you are ready to write the paper. For first time writers, this can be intimidating. Questions that flow through one's head include:

- Where do I start?
- What level should I pitch it at?
- Do I put in this information? Will it be too much information?
- Do I have to reference everything that I write?
- How do I ensure all my important ideas/pertinent points are communicated in the paper?
- How do I write a discussion that has depth?

Just some tips below on how to get started, how to keep it going and get a paper written:

- **Have an outline**

Having an outline makes the whole writing exercise easier as it is like a template for you to fill in the blanks (remember, you already have all the data!). An outline consists of:

- o Title
- o Authors
- o Abstract (Introduction, Objective, Methods, Results, Conclusion, keywords)
- o Introduction/Background
- o Objective/Aims
- o Methods
- o Results
- o Discussion
- o Conclusion
- o Others — Key points, who did what, declare any competing interest, acknowledgement

- Authors — Remember to put in which institution/hospital each author belongs to. Some journals may require you to put in their job title as well.

- Introduction/Background — I usually copy the Introduction/Background from what I have written in my Research Protocol and maybe expand slightly on it. General outline is as below:

  o Start off with a general statement regarding the field/topic of your research and highlight the issues surrounding the topic.

  o State current evidence.

  o Indicate the gap in the current literature and explain why it is important to fill this gap. Interest your readers in the novelty of your work by outlining how your current research can add to existing knowledge.

  o You could also detail the structure of the rest of the paper.

  o Example as below:

    General Statement — Obstructive sleep apnea (OSA) is a condition that has significant impact on patient's long-term health as well as quality of life.
    Current Evidence — Continuous positive airway pressure (CPAP) is the current gold standard treatment. It has been demonstrated to be effective in relieving upper airway obstruction (Engleman *et al.*, 2004) and producing a favourable long-term cardiovascular outcome.

    Issue — However, CPAP compliance remains alarmingly low at around 40%.
    Gap in Literature — Little is known regarding reasons for non-compliance towards CPAP treatment.

    Significance of Your Study — We propose to evaluate the reasons for CPAP failure/non-compliance in patients with OSA. With this evaluation, we hope to be able to address the patient concerns, subsequently improve CPAP compliance in the future and ultimately improve patient outcomes.

Structure — The first part of our study will focus on reasons for non-compliance. The second part of our study will endeavour to assess strategies to enhance compliance.

- Objective — This is pretty self-explanatory; again, you can copy and paste from your Research Protocol. Occasionally, you can have more than one objective in your study. State clearly which are the primary or secondary objectives.

- Methods — It is important to provide enough detail so that readers have a clear understanding of what was done.

  E.g. (Not enough detail) — Lymph node was harvested and stained. (Better version) — Cervical lymph node was harvested from participants under local anaesthesia and stained with the hematoxylin and eosin stain

- You also should detail your sample size calculation if it was done.

- Active or Passive voice — When writing your methods, it doesn't matter which style you choose to write in as long as you are consistent with it. Try not to mix them up, it irritates readers. E.g.

  Active — We obtained participants' baseline blood pressure in the clinic. We also examined their medical records to obtain information regarding their co-morbidities, family history and smoking habits.

  Passive — Participants' baseline blood pressure was obtained in clinic. Medical records of participants were examined for number of co-morbidities, family history and smoking habits.

  Mixed (not encouraged) — We obtained participants' baseline blood pressure in the clinic. Medical records of participants were also examined for the number of co-morbidities, family history and smoking habits.

- Results — Usually start with patient demographics (gender, age range/mean, total number of patients recruited (N), etc.), followed by important findings. It is helpful to provide details. E.g.

If you mention 90% of patients were noted to develop symptoms, try and put in the actual figure of patients in brackets — 90% (88/97) of patients developed symptoms.

RESULTS

There were 7 case series published from 1994 to 2011 on the role of routine chest X-ray in adult surgical tracheostomy. 5 were retrospective and 2 were prospective studies, with a combined total of 1382 cases and 1362 radiographs (**Summary Table 1**); 20 cases did not have post-operative chest X-ray for unspecified reasons. The studies recruited adults of all ages and gender. Based on available data, the age range was from 12 to 93 years, with an average of 58.3 years. Male to female preponderance was unknown. 91

Chest Radiography-Detected Complication Rates

Of the 1382 cases of open surgical tracheostomy, there were only 30 cases (2.2%) with chest X-ray detected complications. This included pneumothorax (9), atelectasis (8), pulmonary oedema (5), pneumomediastinum (5) and subcutaneous emphysema (3). In particular, the rate of pneumothorax was only 0.7% (9/1382). 48

Complications with Chest X-ray Changes that Required Significant Intervention

70% (21/30) of cases with chest X-ray detected complications did not require any intervention, and were managed through observation. 20% (6/30) received conservative treatment (medical therapy or ventilator pressure modifications), while only 10% (3/30) required invasive intervention (tube thoracostomy) (**Figure 1** & **Summary Table 1**). In other words, only 30% (9/30) of chest radiographs with positive findings, or a mere 0.7% (9/1362) of the entire series of chest radiographs performed, have actually led to significant changes on clinical management. 88

- If your results have many subsections, try and insert headings to make it easier for your readers. Example is as above (black arrows):

- Use graphs, tables, schematics, figures to make your paper more palatable.

- Statistical tests used, power and confidence interval should be stated.

- Discussion — Most people stumble at Discussion because the structure, length and discussion points can vary significantly between papers. Points you could discuss include:

  o Explain your findings — you can highlight some of the interesting/important findings and provide plausible explanation for the results. Also consider alternative explanations if available.

  o Compare your results with those in the existing literature — do they contradict or support the existing findings. Try and provide an explanation for the discrepancies between your study and those in the published literature.

  o Strengths and weakness of your study (if there is a weakness in design, you can explain the reason for it and propose ways to circumvent it).

  o State the potential implications and applications of your research finding.

  o Proposal for future studies (what it should include, how it should be designed).

- Conclusion — Dependent on your results/findings. If you are not sure, best ask your supervisor/senior authors.

- Editing — After your first draft, you might want to revise your paper before sending it to your supervisor. This involves re-examining the organisation and flow to ensure coherence. You could also check through your paper for grammar, sentence structure and spelling.

- Refer to other similar articles — reading articles written by other authors gives you an idea about what level to pitch your paper at, how much information to insert, which are the pertinent points that reviewers/readers might be interested in, how to create a logical flow in presenting your results.

- Use simple words, avoid jargon and acronyms. You can use acronyms, but make sure you explain them once at the beginning of the article.

9. Presentation of results/publication

I love this part of research. Presenting your results is like graduation after five years of medical school. It is a show of what you have achieved after all that hard work. Presentation of your results to your department can also raise awareness of your research topic and potentially change practice. There are various platforms for presentation, including:

- Departmental meetings
  - o Continuous Medical Education (CME) sessions, Journal Club, Morbidity or Mortality meetings, Research meetings are platforms at which you can present your research findings.

  - o Ask the organiser of these sessions — usually they will be more than keen to let you present. However, do seek permission from your supervisor prior to presenting.

- Local /regional/international conferences
  - o If you are a house officer/medical officer, e-mails regarding conferences usually get sent out by the hospital or departmental secretaries. Keep your eyes open.

  - o A very good local conference to present at is the yearly Singapore Health & Biomedical Congress (SHBC) — http://www.shbc.com.sg/

  - o If you are not sure which conferences to present at, again, ask your supervisor.

Which Journals?

There are a few considerations in terms of which journals to submit to

- **General versus Specialty-specific journals**
  This depends on who your target audience is — who do you think might be interested in your paper. There are journals with general themes like the *British Medical Journal (BMJ Open)* or *Lancet*, etc. and there are various specialty-specific journals

such as *Clinical Otolaryngology*, the *Journal of Pediatric Psychology*, etc. You might want to ask your supervisor about his or her preference.

There are also various journals which are not specialty themed, but are oriented towards different aspects of medicine, for instance — the *Journal of Education, Journal of Quality Management, Journal of Healthcare Quality, American Journal of Epidemiology*, and the *Journal of Bioethics*, etc. If your paper has relevance to the scope of the journal, it is worth considering.

- **Local versus international journals**

Again, this is dependent on your target audience. If you study is more relevant to the local context or has more implications in the local setting, might be worth considering publication in local journals such as the *Singapore Medical Journal, Singapore Family Physician* journal, *Asian Journal of Surgery*, etc.

- **Impact factor**

Impact factor is a measure of importance of a journal in its field. It is measured based on the average number of citations its articles get. As a general rule, the higher the impact factor, the better the journal, and the harder it is to get an article accepted. Google your journal name + impact factor — most of the time you will find it. Or you could try this website: http://impactfactor.weebly.com/

- **Article format**

It is worth having a look through a journal to see the type of articles they publish before submitting hastily only to be turned down. This is dependent on your study design. For example, not all journals accept Case Reports. In these instances, you may want to submit your case report to either a specialty-specific journal that accepts case reports or journals that specialise in case reports, such as *BMJ Case Reports and International Journal of Surgery Case Reports*.

If you are unsure of which journals to submit your articles to, you could Google similar articles to yours to see where they were published and you might want to try your luck there.

Submission Process

Send your manuscript to the right journal. Make sure your study matches the scope and aims of the journal. Usually this is stated in the journal's website. This is important, as the submission process can be laborious and time consuming. You want to avoid wasting time if you can help it. If it is a match, then you can create an account at the journal website and start your submission process.

Follow the format. Next thing to do is to read through the journal's editorial guide for manuscript preparation (usually under 'instruction for authors') to ensure that your research paper matches the format and illustration style that is required by the journal. Based on that, do the necessary formatting then submit your study.

Be patient + start early. This whole process takes time. The process involves a lot of revision and resubmission, providing explanation for reviewers when they ask for it, obtaining signatures from supervisors/research team members for declaration of competing interests, for acknowledgement of amendments and so on. You may have to go back and forth a few times before the whole deal is done and dusted (that is if your article is accepted at all!). My very first publication took one year from submission to actual print and was not in time for my job application at that time. So, if you hope to have a publication on your CV at the time of Residency application, it would be worth starting early.

What if my paper is rejected? Don't be dejected if your article is rejected (no pun intended) — you have the advantage of feedback. You can revise your paper based on the suggestions of previous reviewers and then resubmit it to another journal. I have had a case report that was rejected three times before finally being accepted by an American journal. Sometimes, you may have to be creative — if your paper is rejected, you may have to re-submit in another format/style that might 'interest' the journal editor. For instance, some journals have sections such as Letter to Editor, Picture Quiz, How We Do It, Snapshot in Surgery, etc. where you might be able to modify your article style to match those sections and submit them.

Tips: How to Get Started on a Research Project?

So now you have a general idea of the research process. The question is — what next? How do I get started?

Below is a list of things you should think through before embarking (pouring your heart and soul and after school/work hours) on a research project. This is speaking from the painful experience of having at least five or six projects that amounted to nothing. Genuinely, these are the things I wish someone had told me when I started off.

1)   Selection of mentor

Mentors are pivotal in your research process, particularly so if it is your first research project. It is likely to determine whether you ultimately produce anything of substance.

I am always reminded of my 4th year medical school elective project. I remembered vividly being enthusiastic enough to start the project 6 months before the start of my elective period. However, my mentor was away for a large part of my elective period. I had no prior research experience, and little guidance. I had plunged straight into data collection. It wasn't until I sat in front of the statistician with my hard slogged data that I was told to my dismay that my sample size was insufficient to achieve any statistical significance. Power calculation should have been done at the start of the project. Given the limited time I had and that my elective report was due soon, I had no choice but to wrap up and produce an elective report from months of hard work, without any publication. It was extremely frustrating.

Conversely, one of my peers who got attached to a professor who had the interest and research experience to guide her through her research project, got herself two first-author publications at the end of her electives.

So, my advice is, do try and obtain some information about your potential supervisor before committing. Useful things to look for are research experience, publications, track record with other students and area of interest. Most supervisors' or consultants' areas of interest (and sometimes CV) are available online/hospital websites.

However, not all professors with many research projects behind their back have time to guide beginners through their first research project. Sometimes, research fellows, registrars, and junior consultants might be able to afford more time to guide you through your project.

Another way to find out, as non-scientific as it is, is through word of mouth. Find out from current residents, medical officers or students who have worked with the respective supervisors as to who is best to get attached to for research projects.

In addition, it would also be ideal to perform research project with the department and institution you intend to apply to for your Residency job. As mentioned previously, it could build rapport, increase your visibility, and the supervisors can potentially act as your referees in your Residency application.

2) Selection of project

It would be ideal for you to do a project in the field of your interest. However, as alluded to earlier, if you cannot make up your mind on what field you want to work in, it would be worth doing your projects on something with a general theme. Ideally, it should the sort of project that interests you (lab work, clinical work, epidemiological type studies, etc.).

Type and length project is very important as well. For your first few projects, it might be worth starting off with something on a smaller scale. Should you manage to complete and present it, it can help give you a confidence boost to move on to bigger projects. Case reports and retrospective studies are good to start off with. This is because you have more control of time, and the likelihood of completion is higher — i.e. you don't have to wait for potential participants to come in to be recruited. Subsequently, you could progress to the more complex and demanding prospective study, which may involve planning of logistics, obtaining of funding and recruitment of patients.

Sure, a student who has a published randomised-controlled trial or systematic review is more impressive than a student that has a published case report. However, having a randomised-controlled trial that is 'in-progress' at the time of application is likely to be less substantial compared to a retrospective study that has be published and presented at conferences. Just because you have something in progress does not mean it will necessarily pan out. In some ways, it may reflect on your lack of planning as well. The idea is to get the whole process completed at the time of application. Of course, this is not absolute and there are exceptions.

If you could, it would be good to get involved and go through the motions of literature search, designing study, ethics application, data collection, data entry, write up, presentation and submission.

3)   Pre-discuss the details

When you meet your supervisor to discuss a potential research project, first be upfront about your own experience. You should send a copy of your CV to the potential supervisor before the meeting and also bring a copy with you for the potential supervisor at your first meeting.

It also helps if you could specify the period for which you are available. Usually students make themselves available during the period of elective/attachment to the department. However, it is always advantageous if you could follow through with the project even after the period of elective (if it is not completed) — i.e. on your own time (but definitely not at the risk of jeopardising your studies/clinical work).

Ideally, authorship should be pre-discussed. I understand this may not be easy from a medical student/junior doctor's stand-point. It can also be a bit too forthcoming for the local culture. In addition, for your first few projects, perhaps the emphasis could be more on the learning experience, rather than authorship.

However, if the situation allows, it can be useful being upfront. But do note that this has to be handled with good EQ and sensitiv-ity. Depending on the situation and context, you could perhaps pre-discuss with your supervisor about your aims (such as to be first/second author, to be able to present the paper in a conference as a first author, etc.), and ask what needs to be done in order to achieve that. But also have the sensitivity to understand that your supervisor is likely to have a more comprehensive overview of the whole process and project to be able to decide. Hence, if your request gets rejected, you need to respect your supervisor's deci-sion and don't be too disappointed. Regardless of authorship, you will still be able to learn and gain something through the project. Also, understand that if you ask to be the first/second author, you need to make sure you have the means to live up to it and put in the work required. It would reflect badly if you ask for a lot and don't deliver. It can leave a bad impression and affect your Residency application.

Delineate your role — ask clear questions about what you are expected to do — literature search, design study, ethics applica-tion, data collection, data entry, data analysis, write up, submis-sion. Ideally, you'd want to be involved in all steps above in order to gain experience.

4) Set out your aims

- Try to get a few things done with the research project

    - Local departmental presentation, e.g. departmental journal club/research meeting. Departmental presentations, although less impactful on your CV compared to local/international conferences, are useful in increasing your presence within the department (I call it 'face time') — which may have an impact on Mopex application for rotation in the department/residency application.

    - Poster/oral presentation at local or international conferences (before submitting to respective conferences, always obtain permission from the supervisor/senior author)
    - Publication in a peer-reviewed journal

- Outline your intentions and the aims of the project to your potential supervisors

5) Maintain clear communication

- It is crucial to maintain clear communication with your supervisors.
- That means returning e-mails promptly as well as giving your supervisor an update from time to time regarding your progress with the research project (even when not prompted).

- There will be times where you meet your supervisors for discussion. I tend to write an e-mail to the supervisor to summarise all things discussed and subsequent plans/things to do. I think this serves as a reminder to myself, and is always a useful reference to keep your research progress in check .

6) Stats consult (!)

If I haven't emphasized this enough — it is advisable that you consult a statistician regarding power analysis and sample size estimation before you embark on a research project. This is applicable if you intend to run a statistical test in your research project later.

I will be honest and admit that I have no idea how to do this myself and am heavily reliant on statisticians to help provide an accurate estimation of sample size for my study. Trust me, taking the effort to arrange the appointment and finding time to get there pays. It is always helpful to send your research protocol to the statistician prior to your meeting so that they have time to read through and understand your research project.

It is also helpful if you could source out and print out previous similar studies (if available) for their reference. It helps them put your research project into context and provide estimation of your sample size to help achieve statistical significance.

7) See it through

After you get started, try your best to see the research project through. Often there will be factors out of your control. However, try as much as you can to drive the research process. Your supervisor may not have the time to remind you to proceed with the next step. From your prior discussion with your supervisor, as well as steps outlined in the research process above, you should have an idea of what needs to be done next, so get going with it. For instance, when one starts with data collection, it would be always good to start designing and setting up a data entry table (Microsoft Excel/Microsoft Access/SPSS). If you could draft one up and send it to your supervisor (without being asked), it shows initiative.

Set a timeline with your supervisor as to when to achieve the different milestones. Try and keep track of this timeline and send gentle non-intrusive reminders to your supervisors or other parties involved when things are delayed. However, all should be done within reasonable means, obviously (ahem). Try and avoid over aggressive pestering which could backfire.

Always try and make it easy for the other parties involved. If your supervisor is too busy to reply to your e-mail about the questions you have about the project, it might be worth trying to catch them after rounds as they are sitting down for breakfast with the rest of the team, or as they are walking towards clinic/theatre, or simply just whichever time that is most convenient for them (ask them).

I used to print the draft of my write-up for my supervisor to read in between theatre cases. With this I got the correction of my draft done within a day, after weeks of un-replied e-mails.

In Summary

Research can be a pain, especially when done under pressure to check tick-boxes in the application for training jobs. It can be daunting, with the number of hurdles and hoops to jump through, as well as the uncertainties that await. However, occasionally you will come across some new discovery or development, or something that can impact clinical practice and change things, something that will make it worthwhile. Or sometimes it is just the pride of simply realising that you know the subject and evidence well in your discussion with your colleagues, or even just understanding statistics better during the journal club discussion. Look on the bright side. Have faith. 'Don't get discouraged; it is often the last key in the bunch that opens the lock.' — Unknown.

References

Aslam F, Shakir M, Qayyum MA. (2005) Why Medical Students Are Crucial to the Future of Research in South Asia. *PLoS Med* **2(11):** e322. [http://www.plosmedicine.org/article/info%3Adoi%2F10.1371%2Fjournal.pmed.0020322-]

Detsky ME, Detsky AS. (2007) Encouraging medical students to do research and write papers. *CMAJ* **176(12):** 1719–1721. [http://www.ecmaj.ca/content/176/12/1719.full]

Aslam S, Emmanuel P. (2010) Formulating a researchable question: A critical step for facilitating good clinical research. *Indian J Sex Transm*

Dis **31(1):** 47–50. [http://www.ncbi.nlm.nih.gov/pmc/articles/PMC3140151/]

Sackett D, Richardson WS, Rosenburg W, Haynes RB. (1997) *How to Practice and Teach Evidence Based Medicine* (2nd edn.). Churchill Livingstone.

Hulley SB, Cummings SR, Browner WS, *et al.* (2007) *Designing Clinical Research* (3rd edn.). Lippincott Williams and Wilkins.

Rohrig B, du Prel JB, Blettner M. (2009) Study Design in Medical Research. *Dtsch Arztebl Int* **106(11):** 184–189. http://www.ncbi.nlm.nih.gov/pmc/articles/PMC2695375/

Kellestinova ED. (2001) How to Write Your First Research Paper. *Yale Journal of Biology and Medicine* **84(3):** 181–190.

Data management http://cctsi.ucdenver.edu/RIIC/Pages/DataManagement.aspx

5

How to Do Presentations

"There is no such thing as talent, it is called Presentation Skills."
— David JP Phillips

"Sometimes, it is not about what you know, it is about what you can show about what you kn technique ow." — Unknown

> **Key Points**
> - Being able to present your findings in an easy to comprehend, logical manner is essential for effective communication with patients and colleagues.
> - Good presentation skills allows effective diffusion of information at patient forums, departmental presentations, and conferences/scientific meetings.
> - To deliver an effective presentation — know your topic well, pitch at the right level, provide an outline and summary, ensure adequate flow and coherence between your slides, entice your audience with a storyline and use keywords.
> - Take time to prep well — always rehearse your presentation.

Why are Presentation Skills Important?

This is very much an entry-level quick points on how to do oral presentations. Its relevance to Residency is in the fact that as a resident, as with most doctors, you will be required to do presentations frequently. Being able to present your findings in a logical, easy to comprehend manner is essential for effective communication with patients and colleagues. Presentation skills are important for a variety of settings:

- Patient forums — when disseminating information to the public and performing patient education.
- Departmental meetings — presenting audit findings, discussing journal papers.
- Conferences and scientific meetings — presenting research findings.

In addition, oral presentations aid in creating a presence within the department which could help in the process of getting a residency post.

How to Do a Good Presentation

1) **Know your topic well**
    - First, get your facts and figures correct, make sure they are up to date, and quote your sources.

    - Know your content well, for example:

        o For presentation of your research project — be sure you are aware of current literature and how your study complements the existing knowledge.

        o Understand and be able to explain the purpose behind your chosen methods.

        o Be able to explain why a certain statistical test was used, and what the statistical significance implies.

- o Be especially clear about your results, have every fact and figure at your fingertips. You should be able to explain missing data/study drop outs/anomalies.

- o For discussions — make sure you are aware of the strengths and shortcomings of your research study. Try and quote other similar papers and compare the findings with your own study.

2) **Read around periphery/relevant topics/landmark papers**

- Reading relevant topics helps you figure out what to say during the presentation and adds depth to your presentation.

- It can also help put your presentation into perspective for your audience.

- For instance, prior to presenting on my research on 'Flexible nasoendoscope decontamination with Chlorine Dioxide' (a study I did in the UK on the effectiveness of the decontamination agent for ENT flexible nasoendoscopes) to the Department of ENT Surgery at Tan Tock Seng Hospital, I spent time reading up on locally used decontamination agents even though they were not part of my research.

- I then added a slide comparing my research findings on Chlorine Dioxide with local decontamination agents. I discussed various aspects including evidence of efficacy, costs, and pros and cons of both, which helped put my study into the local context, and helped my audience understand the relevance of my study to the local healthcare setting.

- Another example — when I presented in a Journal Club session on the management of Bell's palsy (idiopathic facial palsy), I discussed the landmark paper published in the *New England Journal of Medicine* on Bell's palsy in 2004. It earned me a few nods from the consultants in the department for demonstrating awareness and ability to keep abreast of recent developments in the field.

- Admittedly, it can sometimes be difficult to read extensively about a topic owing to the pressure of time. There are still times where my presentations were suboptimal because of lack of time to read around the topic.

- In addition, at a junior level, without being in the field long enough, one sometimes lacks the peripheral knowledge to be able to gauge what the audience might be interested in, as well as to know about recent developments/landmark papers. Hence, it is usually helpful to get someone more senior than you, usually a friendly registrar or a consultant, to look through your presentation and to give you suggestions on the points above.

3) **Pitch at the right level (know your audience)**

- Tailor the talk to audience. Pitch your talk at the correct level. Try to think in the sense of, if you were the audience, what you would like to know, how can you make the presentation useful for the audience?

- For instance, on the topic of 'Obstructive Sleep Apnea', what I would talk about depends on who my audience is.

  a) Medical Students: Definition of obstructive sleep apnea, physiology of obstructive sleep apnea, Epworth Sleepiness Scale, how to take a history, how to do clinical examination, etc. Generally, more basic sciences.

  b) Junior doctors: Investigation and treatment modalities of obstructive sleep apnea, American Academy of Sleep Medicine Clinical Guidelines for Obstructive Sleep Apnea, current evidence.

  c) Consultants: Recent developments in the field and evidence.

  o Sometimes there is a mixed audience. In such situations it would be best to pitch your presentation at the majority or tailor it to the setting of the talk. For instance, in a departmental meeting, attended by medical students and doctors — the majority of the audience would be house officers, medical officers, registrars and consultants — I would then have only one or two slides on basic sciences/background, then move on to the current guidelines and evidence.

4) **Outline and summary**

- Having an outline gives your audience an overview of what you will be talking about, thus making it easier for the audience to understand and follow your talk.

- This also helps in creating a flow for your talk and helps give a sense of consistency throughout the talk.

- The 'Summary' slide is used as a 'take-home message' to drive your points across.

- In addition to a summary at the end of your presentation, you can also do a short summary in between different sections of your talk, especially if your presentation is very long.

- It can help the audience recap and recall the pertinent points in the talk and elicit interesting discussion in the ensuing Q&A/discussions.

5) **What to say?**

- What you say during your presentation is important to entice your audience into the 'story' of your presentation. Using transition words, adjectives and emphasis helps connect one idea to the next, provide coherence and draw your audience' attention to various pertinent points in your presentation.

- Below are some transition words that you can use in your presentation to create flow:

  o Additive transition — in addition, moreover, further to my original point, besides, in fact, let alone, not to mention this

- o Clarification — by this I mean, to explain, that is to say
- o Emphasis — above all, most importantly
- o Conflict — however, conversely, on the other hand, contrary to this
- o Result — as a result/consequence, consequently, hence, therefore
- o Sequential — to start/begin with, first of all, followed by, subsequently, next

- Use keywords — Word choice is important to help you draw the attention of your audience. For instance:
  - o this is a 'significant' finding in our study... interesting, puzzling, amazing, extraordinary
  - o Now. I'd like to move on to the most important slide of the whole presentation
  - o I would like to draw your attention to this finding...

- Explain your graphs — what is this graph about? What does the x-axis represent, what does the y-axis represent, what does each bar/colour mean. Many people tend to just flash a slide containing the graph and expect the audience to understand it at a glance. I certainly am not quick enough to do that. Taking the effort to explain (if time allows) and putting it into context for your audience can help demonstrate eloquence and shows that you are considerate.

- Give meaning to the statistics — what does it mean, how does it relate clinically.

6) Connect with your audience + build rapport

- Connect with your audience by telling them the relevance of your presentation to them.
  - o 'So, how does that relate to YOUR practice? How is it different/similar to YOUR current practice? How does this change what we do?'

- o 'As we know, in our department, Prof X usually performs... this paper illustrates a modification of Prof's technique. How Prof does it is... how the authors in this paper differ is by...'

- o 'Remember last month, we had a lecture from our visiting expert on... our presentation today represents a different school of thought, and I am about to illustrate it with the evidence that we have gathered.'

- Appeal to your audience by speaking their minds.

  - o 'I know it's late and a lot of you are rushing to go home. So I will make this presentation short and sweet.'

  - o 'I sense a lot of you are puzzled with this finding, but allow me to explain.'

- Be able to mock things/yourself.

  - o Steve Jobs in his commencement address to Stanford Class of 2005 said: 'I've never graduated from college. This is the closest I have ever got to graduation.' This sort of irony is endearing, earnest and funny. It immediately drew the crowd to his side.

- Be controversial (in a not too controversial way)

  - o 'The shocking truth is, what we thought we knew has been WRONG all along. Let me explain why.'

  - o 'Ladies and gentlemen, you are in for a treat. Today I am going to disprove Einstein's theories one by one before you.'

  - o Nothing catches attention like a bit of shit stirring. You cause commotion by poking fun at something and revealing information to get reaction. By doing so, you get attention for your presentation. Though, word of advice — this one is slightly dangerous and can backfire. Only do it if you have the charm to pull it off and if you have the solid data to back you up.

- Get personal
  - ○ 'Before I start this presentation, I'm going to tell you my life story.'

7) Rehearse, rehearse and rehearse

- It is never enough just to prepare your PowerPoint slides and then 'just look at the slides and talk lah' on the day of the presentation. The converse is true. One should not be monotonously reading off stacks of cue cards.

- By rehearsing, one should try to achieve a level where your slides, what you say and how you present gel synergistically — offering your audience a sense that you know your stuff, you are engaging, and you are confident in what you are talking about.

- The late Steve Jobs, one of the most captivating presenters in the world, practiced hundreds of hours prior to his presentations. That probably explains why he was always so sleek and effortless when presenting at all the Apple product launches.

- If you've never watched a Steve Jobs presentation, I would highly recommend that you try watching one — his iPhone launch presentation was exemplary.

- This deliberate repeated practice allows you to refine the things that you say, and make purposeful pauses or gestures, making your presentation succinct, logical yet engaging, thereby making it an effective presentation.

- I have very fond memories of one of the best presentations I have delivered — for which I won the prize for Best Oral Presentation at the North of England Otolaryngology Society meeting in 2011.

- I still remember very vividly the rigour and drilling that my consultant, Mr. Karagama, put me through when rehearsing for that presentation. Just to show you how mad we were about rehearsing, we spent no less than 30 minutes perfecting (just) my opening line.

- This is what my opening slide looks like.

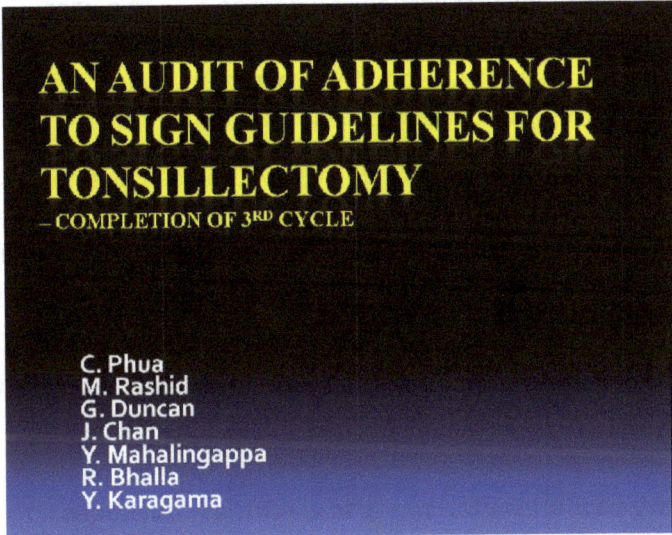

- This was my first take on the opening line: 'A very good morning to everyone. My name is Chu Qin. I am an ENT Core Trainee from Tameside General Hospital, Manchester. Today I would like to present to you an audit that we performed in our hospital on 'An Audit of Adherence to SIGN Guidelines for Tonsillectomy — a completion of the 3rd cycle.'

- Notice how incredibly long winded I was. I was giving a lot of unnecessary information and bored the audience by reading off the slide.

- There were no less than 15 various attempts and rehearsals in between (just for an opening line!). Mr. Karagama (bless him!) made multiple corrections to the words I used, my emphasis on different words, my tone, and even the amount of enthusiasm of which I was displaying.

- This was the final line: 'Hi, I am Chu Qin. Today, I'd like to **share** with you our audit on Tonsillectomy, which I am sure you would find **most relevant** to your day to day practice.'

- Notice how more succinct and effective the last line is, compared to the first version. It works on a more personal level, and seeks to captivate the audience members' attention by telling them this is something pertinent to their day-to-day practice, which deserves their attention.

- As I have learnt, you don't have to read out the whole title — that's what your visual aid (slide) is for. The audience can read it themselves. But if you don't spend time rehearsing and listening to how you sound, you will not be able to refine it this way.

- Refining what you say helps sustain your audience's attention and helps you deliver your points more effectively.

8) Vary your presentation — use videos, ask questions

- Varying your presentation helps in sustaining your audience's attention. It can be done via a variety of ways — inserting videos, asking questions, etc.

- I once sat through a Head and Neck cancer forum, chaired by Dr. Choo Bok Ai, Consultant Radiation Oncologist, NUH. Forums are traditionally dull and mainly consisted of didactic presentations and information giving. However, Dr. Choo started the forum by doing a presentation with a Q&A on Head and Neck cancers. It was some trivia on Head and Neck cancers, and prizes were given out for correct answers. He had the crowd roaring with laughter and excitement. More importantly, he used the Q&A to illustrate to the audience the importance of Head and Neck cancer information, hence setting the scene for the subsequent presentations. As a result, the audience was more upbeat and partook actively in subsequent sessions.

- Although, it has to be said, not everyone has the ability or charm to pull off something like this. So, if you are about to pull a stunt like this, try and make sure you are in a position to do it.

9) **Personalise your presentation**

- Adding a personal touch to the presentation usually helps leave an impression on your audiences.
- Some of my UK professors like to start talk with some history and trivia related to their topic.

  Some would use celebrities to illustrate conditions. For instance, one of the diabetes talks, a consultant flashed up pictures of Tom Hanks, Nick Jonas and Halle Berry, and then asked us what these celebrities had in common.

- One of the presentations which left a striking impression in me was done by Dr. Edwin Seet, Consultant Anaesthetist, KTPH. It was one of the compulsory hospital talks on safety in hospital practice.

  It was a very dry topic but at the end of the talk, I was glad I dragged myself out of bed for it.

- Instead of doing a 'you should do this and you shouldn't do this' talk, Dr. Seet illustrated the importance of Safety in Hospital Practice with the 'Pareto principle', backed with evidence and figures to illustrate his point. The Pareto principle states that about 80% of effects come from 20% of the causes. Translated into the healthcare setting, 20% of hazards in the healthcare setting account for 80% of the injuries/sequelae. This highlighted the importance of hazard prioritisation. Hence, by spending our resources and energy targeting and ensuring safety in practice, we stand to prevent a large chunk of complications and sequelae. It made logical and economic sense to me and completely won me over.

- You can see from the examples above that it wasn't just the usual bog standard fact sharing/regurgitating session. By adding these little snippets (whilst maintaining relevance to your talk), you stand to impress your audience, some of whom could be your interviewers, consultants, or training programme directors.

- However, truthfully, my (humble) opinion is that learning how to personalise your talk is something to be considered only after you've mastered the initial points illustrated above. At the level of a junior doctor, it is more important for one to first get the content and flow right. Thereafter, you could choose to work on how to personalise your talk.

- But remember, you could personalise your talk whichever way you want. It doesn't have to follow the mould of the examples that I have given here. It can be whatever subject dear to your heart. However make sure there is some **relevance** to your presentation or that it illustrates a point. Also, make sure you have the means to pull it off.

10) Dealing with questions

- Often at the end of the presentation there will be a Q&A session. To most people this is a nightmare. I still get sweaty palms now and again when it comes to this section.

- Pre-empt and anticipate: Try and pre-empt the questions by reading around the topic. Try and sit with your supervisor/ friendly senior and forecast some questions and prepare the answers.

- To buy time so that you can organise your answer.

  o Acknowledge and credit the person — 'This is a good question, I am glad you asked this.'

  o Repeat the question and ask 'Do I understand you correctly'. It gives you an extra minute to think and formulate your answer. It also helps ensure that the rest of the audience heard the question and are able to follow the discussion.

- If you have the answer in one of your previous slides, flip to that slide and illustrate your answer with the aid of your slide.

- A couple of good 'get off the hook' lines:
  - o 'I am afraid this isn't within the scope of our study, but thank you for the suggestion. This is something that we could certainly look into later.'
  - o 'I am not sure I have the answer to this. What we do know in our existing study is this...... Does anyone in the audience have anything to comment?'
  - o 'Well, I have to be honest and admit that I don't have the answer to this. Why don't I look it up and get back to you later?'

11) On the day of the presentation

- Arrive early at conference/meeting venue.

- Make sure your presentation is loaded on the computer and run through it once before the meeting/conference starts.

- Test out your slides, run through them, see if your slides/ graphs/table are decipherable from the end of the hall/conference room. Make adjustments if time allows.

- I sometimes bring my own laptop just in case the computer provided at the venue does not play my presentation properly.

- Back up your presentation on another thumb drive or laptop. Remember Murphy's Law.

- Get familiar with the devices before your presentation — how to clip the mic/switch it on, how to use the pointer, how to move from slide to slide. You'd be surprised how fiddly these things are, especially when you are presenting under stress. It would just look much sleeker if you are able to get things like that under control and appearing effortless.

12) Other tips

- Font — use a font that is decipherable from the end of the hall.

- Colour — use a different colour to emphasis keywords.

- Crowding — Don't crowd slides. If your slide is too wordy or has too many bullet points, people tend to lose attention. Try and divide them into different slides. If you absolutely must put them into one slide, try and highlight the pertinent points/keywords in colour or underline them, which will help your audience speed read and capture their attention.

- Don't squeeze in too much information — details can be given during the Q&A session or illustrated in your final paper publication.

- With each slide — have a purpose. Don't waste your slides. The moment you talk about something non-relevant, people lose interest and doze off.

- Have more (relevant) pictures and graphs to illustrate your point.

- Use other non-verbal communications — gestures, animations on slides, or use a laser pointer to emphasise points.

- Repetition — to drive points in (of course, without overdoing it and annoying your audience).

- Quote evidence — put in graphs/tables from journal papers.

- Go slow. Project your voice clearly.

In Summary

All in all, it takes practice to become good. Keep going at it and learn from it each time. I certainly had a lot of help and pointers when I first started doing these presentations. In addition, I also took inspiration from various fantastic speakers that I came across. So, at your next conference/meeting where someone else is presenting, (in addition to the content) try and take note of what was good about their presentation style and maybe you could try and apply it in your next talk. Good luck with your next presentation!

6

How to Write Personal Statements

"First say to yourself what you would be and then do what you have to do." ~Epictetus~

Key Points

- Personal statement is a chance for you to paint a profile of who you are to your selection committee
- Use your personal statements to showcase your intent and interest towards the specialty. Highlight your strengths.
- Avoid generic statements
- Try and elaborate or provide examples to back up your statements
- Get someone to proofread your personal statement prior to submission

The personal statement is part of the application to the Residency Program. It is not something that is looked at in isolation; rather, it is evaluated along with a string of other things — like your CV, performances in previous rotations, qualifications and so on. It is a chance for you to convince your interviewers/selectors what a 'good fit' you are with the Residency Program. It also gives you a chance to paint a profile of who you are and to let your personality shine through.

However, personal statements are akin to the interview question — 'Tell me about yourself'. It is frustrating to say the least. It is so free-styled that you wonder where to start — What do I say? What do they expect me to say? How do I best showcase myself? Are there any tick-boxes, or brownie points that I can earn along the way?

It is always challenging to write a personal statement, particularly when you want to showcase your best self in a very limited word count.

Key Points in a Personal Statement

- Paint a brief background — education, jobs that led to the current interest in the specialty

- Showcase your interest and intent to join the specialty
  - What has drawn you to this specialty? what are its characteristics that attracted you? Any event that has led to this interest?

  - Try not to make generic statements like "I like Orthopaedics because it is interesting and I can help people"

  - If you were to make generic statements, elaborate slightly and back it up by illustrating examples of your own clinical experience. For instance, "I like Orthopaedicas because it is interesting and I can help people. I find great interest in the intricacies and physics of restoring functions of the limbs and joints. In my four months of Orthopaedics posting, I found great joy in seeing the patients regain mobility and function after surgery."

- Highlight your understanding of the specialty and what it entails to be a specialist in that field

- State the work you've done and effort you've put in to work towards the specialty
  - What have you done to show your commitment towards the specialty — relevant clinical experiences/courses/exams

- Demonstrate what you have learnt from various experiences that you detailed in your CV

- Highlight your drive, work ethic, initiative, thoughts, maturity

- What skills do you have that make you indispensable? What are the personal characteristics that make you a good fit? What can you bring to the table?

- Why does this specific Residency Program represent the best that you are looking for?

- Draw the assessors/interviewers into your world by showcasing a part of your personality

- Your future plans and goals

Dissection of a Personal Statement

With the word limit, it is important to make sure that each sentence in your personal statement counts. To illustrate, I think it is best that we go through an example. Here is a personal statement I wrote for my ENT Residency application.

Thank you for considering my application for this specialty that I am most passionate about. I am a person who has gone the extra mile and will continue to do so in order to be successful in ENT Surgery.

- Shows enthusiasm

- Sets a confident tone and asserts that I want the job

My passion for ENT stemmed from my medical school experience in ENT Surgery. I found the ENT case mix so stimulating and the surgery so challenging that I looked forward to going to the wards and theatres to learn new things every day. This incited so much interest in me that I actively applied for an ENT rotation for my Foundation Year program. I have never looked back since.

- Showcase of trigger/inspiration towards interest for the specialty. No fanciful story. Just an honest, realistic, non-exaggerated statement.

- Showcase of pursuit in your interest, as well as active steering of career.

In working towards becoming an ENT Specialist, I worked hard to create a strong foundation of knowledge by passing the MRCS and DOHNS. I have also attended numerous ENT courses including FESS and Phonosurgery course to strengthen my surgical skills

- Slight rehash of CV, but with explanation of the purpose of each item. Therefore it shows insight and understanding of prerequisites for the specialty. It also demonstrates effort and engagement towards the specialty.

and consolidate my clinical experiences. This, in combination, gave me the confidence in attending to sick patients in ENT, as well as enhanced the enjoyment of my clinical work. In addition, I also benefitted from the Leadership Course, How to Be an OSCE Examiner Course and Good Clinical Practice Research Course which helped me become an all-rounded clinician.

I keep abreast of the developments in ENT by performing research and obtaining publications.

I have made a conscious decision to return to Singapore for work for both personal and professional reasons. I want to be closer to my family and also believe Singapore to be a conducive environment to further my surgical career. Having only worked in the UK since graduation, I am well aware of the challenges ahead, including the difference in culture and workload. Through realistic

• Highlight of other facets that I have developed, e.g. leadership and teaching skills. It also conveys the impression of maturity in having considered other qualities/skills beyond clinical work. It can also be a potential selling point that sets me apart.

• Again, demonstrating effort towards specialty. But no details as it is available in CV + there is a word limit.

• Earnest and personal account of reasons for choosing Singapore.

discussions with my medical colleagues who are currently working in Singapore, I feel I am prepared for it given that I am versatile and keen to learn. In fact, this increase in workload will be beneficial for my stage of training in helping me gain more surgical experience, which I most strongly yearned for during my training years in UK.

I am someone who knows to seize the opportunity and able to perform under pressure, as shown in my achievement in winning the Best Oral Presentation prize at the Registrar's Paper section of the North of England Otolaryngology Society Meeting, despite being the only medical officer among all other Registrars to present. I also contributed topics to the book *Essential Surgery for Finals* when offered the chance to do so by my consultant.

One of my strengths is that I am highly passionate about teaching and I have

- Demonstrates that this career path is well thought out and that I have a realistic view of what lies ahead.

- A description of personal strengths that can help me overcome the challenges.

- An account of why this place/program offers the best of what I am looking for (also a bit of sucking up, lah).

- Highlighting my (biggest) achievements and how they are relevant towards the specialty.

- More boasting. But you get the point.

- This is not just a bland statement of 'I did what'. In stating that I proposed and good organisational skills. I proposed and organised an 'ENT Updates course' for GP Consultants which gave me the experience of inviting speakers, obtaining a venue and purchasing mannequins for the course as well as enhancing my teamwork skills as the course organiser. I co-organised the Medic Insight Program, which is a regional work-placement program aimed at providing pre-med students with insight into Medicine. I also taught at formal ENT Teaching Days for medical students, house officers, and medical officers. I am confident that these skills and experience will come in useful in this field of ENT.

Outside Medicine, I am also a balanced individual as evidenced by my extra-curricular activities such as completing the <u>Tour Du Montblanc Mountain</u> Hike and representing the university in badminton tournaments.

organised the course, it shows drive, initiative and organisational skills.

• Organising a work placement program and doing formal teaching demonstrate affinity for teaching, which is a valuable attribute in medicine.

• Showcasing self as a well-balanced individual who has a life outside medicine. This can be potential conversation starter during interview as well.

Of course, there are other facets that I would have liked to elaborate on if the word limit wasn't an issue. For instance, I could have inserted some anecdotes of clinical encounters that affirmed my career choice or further illustrated why I am a good fit for the program and the program for me. However, one just has to work within the limitations. So, the key thing is to prioritise and put in the highlights among your achievements. The strength of the personal statement above is that it is succinct and demonstrates intent and effort towards the specialty.

Below are links to samples of personal statements. You will notice the writing styles vary, some being more enticing than others. However, the essence of what they are trying to convey remains the same.

- http://www.usmleweb.com/showarticleef.html
- https://career.ucsf.edu/sites/career.ucsf.edu/files/Medical%20 Residency%20Personal%20Statement%20Dissected%20 Sample1.pdf

Dos and Don'ts of Personal Statement

Below is a guide on some dos and don'ts in writing personal statements.

Dos

- Show commitment.
- Show direction — show that you have thought about this career and have actively done things to find out about it.
- Show that you have thought about the options and alternatives, you have insight into what this job is about, and have done things to actively find out about it.
- Demonstrate your strengths/admirable attributes.

- Be persuasive, convince them you deserve the place. Distinguish yourself from other applicants.

- Prove your value/niche, e.g. academic, clinical, research, leadership, organisational abilities, teaching achievements, creativity.

- Put in genuine sentiments, compelling stories to back your descriptive comments about yourself.

- Have a logical flow.

- Get someone to read through your personal statement and give you feedback.

Don'ts

- Don't do general, beauty-pageant-style, empty statements, e.g. 'I would like to become a doctor because I like to heal and help the world become a better place'.

- Do not be too specific about your career plans. The program likes to think it knows what is best for you. They also might want the opportunity to help discover your potential and help guide your development. A student once asked me if it is advisable to declare outright that he wants to do facial plastics in his intention in joining ENT. I think to declare at this very early stage can be slightly precocious and show slightly rash judgement. For one, you have barely started, you have hardly experienced the specialty. You might just appear slightly in over your head by being so sure you want to head into a specific subspecialty. Nonetheless, if the subspecialty you are hoping to venture into is under-subscribed and you have strong case to support your choice (e.g. prior solid clinical experience, research, a PhD, etc.), it can work in your favour.

- Do not put in irrelevant personal facts — the question to ask yourself/to explain to your reader is 'so what'. If you state some fact, e.g. you love playing video games and are one of the board-certified gamers invited by Nintendo to test and design games, this is meaningless unless you use it to illustrate a point. E.g. your affinity for and talent in video games demonstrates great hand–eye coordination that can be an asset in surgical training.

- Avoid eccentric humour. Humour in the right setting can be entertaining and can leave an impression. However, it can risk you being discredited or taken less seriously. It can be splendidly good, or spectacularly bad.

- Avoid acronyms. Avoid repetition.

In Summary

There is no single best format for personal statements. This is perhaps the fun part of it because it allows you to be creative about the ways in which you can profile yourself. Make it an interesting read for your interviewers/readers, incite their interest in you and make them want to know you better. Construct, connect and make yourself a competitive applicant!

7

The Interview

"Sometimes, it is not about what you know, it is about what you can show about what you know." — Unknown

"One important key to success is self-confidence. An important key to self-confidence is preparation." — Arthur Ashe

Key Points

- Interviews in the Residency selection process includes the Multiple Mini Interview (MMI) and the Departmental Interview.
- MMI consists for 4 mini interviews with different case scenarios lasting 10 minutes each.
- Applicants are assessed on their team-working ability, communication skills, compassion, ethical conduct and personal attributes.

> • A useful framework to answer the interview question is the STAR technique: **S**ituation, **T**ask, **A**ction and **R**esponse.
> • Preparation is key. Prior to the interview, try and do mock interviews with your colleagues.

Interviews are part of the Residency selection process. Interviews can be divided into

1) Multiple Mini Interview (MMI)
2) Departmental Interview

Multiple Mini Interview is an interview held by MOH Holdings (MOHH) at a national level. Applicants are required to pass the MMI stage before being submitted for the matching process, where the applicants' preference of speciality and sponsoring institutions will be matched to that of the sponsoring institutions. Departmental Interview is carried out by certain subspecialities in certain institutions to screen their applicants further. The format of the interview differs for different departments.

This chapter aims to provide you with an insight into the MMI process and hopefully arm you with strategies for effective interview preparation.

Interview Format

The current residency interview is in the format of 'Multiple Mini Interviews'. This represents a major change in the selection process which understandably causes anxiety among candidates.

MMI is a scenario-based interview with short structured interview questions. It is not really intended to test your clinical knowledge (although it will require some), rather it is to evaluate non-cognitive factors — which are a set of behaviours, skills, thought processes and strategies which have been shown to predict success in school and work performance. Let's face it — at this stage where candidates are selected for interview, there is no lack of academic prowess. Therefore, this interview format sets out to evaluate other characteristics such as teamwork and collegiality, communication skills, compassion, professional and ethical conduct, personal attributes, motivation, perseverance, self-regulation, social skills, creativity and other such 'soft' skills, which are considered as important in determining employment outcomes.

This assessment is carried out via case scenarios where you are asked how you would handle various situations. Some interviewers might ask you to explain how you would manage the problem, and some scenarios might require role play. Candidates go through four stations, each lasting about 10 minutes. Each station will have one or two interviewers.

The intention of the process is to select individuals who demonstrate capability and flexibility in the patient care, problem solving, continuous self-directed learning and teamwork. In essence, they are trying to select individuals who will thrive in the Residency setting.

Your response is then assessed on domains and traits including (but not limited to):

a)   Teamwork and collegiality
b)   Communication skills
c)   Compassion
d)   Professional and ethical conduct
e)   Personal attributes

(Information above available from Residency website: http://www. physician.mohh.com.sg/medicine/residency/faqs

It is during this process that the interviewers assess your 'communication, reasoning, ethos and problem solving skills'. Answers are scored according to a set rating scale.

Your goal:

1) Demonstrate that you are are a safe doctor and that you know your limitations
2) Demonstrate that you are reliable and have integrity
3) Demonstrate logical thinking and maturity
4) Demonstrate a systematic approach to solving problems
5) Demonstrate that you are able to consider the situation from various perspectives
6) Demonstrate cultural sensitivity and ability to relate to others

Interview techniques

Having a framework in answering your questions is very important. It helps you formulate a logical and coherent answer and stops you from digressing. In addition, it will help you cover all points and bases, as well as appear systematic.

The 'STAR' technique

One of the techniques that I used frequently is the STAR technique. The STAR technique is a good technique to structure and present your answers. It gives you headings which you can expand on and further illustrate.

S — Situation	You should do a quick summary of the scenario given, followed by identification of the issues/specific ethical concerns that arise in the case scenario described.
	E.g. 'From my understanding, this case describes a doctor with an alcohol abuse problem which is affecting his work. The key issue here is to ensure patient safety whilst providing help for the doctor in question.'
	It would be useful to provide some justification for your argument/ analysis of the issues (ideally from various perspectives), rather than just stating them. It is also useful to provide references from various guidelines, but make sure you have your facts correct.
	'E.g. This is a violation of the Singapore Medical Council ethical code and guideline because...'

T — Task	The task is what you need to accomplish or achieve. Just a brief description of your objective will do. You could also sum up the potential challenges which might hinder you from completing your task.
A — Action	Action is where you explain what you would do to solve the problem. If there is more than one step required to solve the problem, try and be sequential. If there is more than one approach to solve the problem, outline it first, then expand further. E.g. 'The treatment of nasal polyps can be medical or surgical. Medical treatment involves...'
	Spend some time explaining the **rationale** behind your action as well. Providing a quality argument/justification is important to help express your view and allows the interviewer to understand the reasoning behind your course of action.
	Rather than just saying 'I would speak to the colleague in question to tell him to stop alcohol abuse', you could say 'I would first approach the colleague in question in a confidential manner to see if he is having any troubles. This would help maintain his dignity and hopefully put him more at ease in talking about the problem. I would then broach the subject of his alcohol abuse and explain how we are concerned that it is affecting his work.'
R — Results/ Review	Describe the outcome/prediction of outcome that might result from your action and make a review on how you can learn from it or improve further. This section also allows you to sum up your case scenario and make a conclusion from it.

There will be some case illustration using the STAR technique in the sample interview questions in the next section.

Useful keywords

Using the right action words will aid in the presentation of your answers and help you express yourself better. Rather than saying 'I **told** the consultant what the patient wants', it sounds better if you say 'I **conveyed** the patient's wishes to the consultant'.

However, be careful not to use superfluous words as it risks being pretentious and distracting. Some useful buzz words:

Communication	Learning	Organising	Leadership	Teamwork
address	attribute	assemble	achieve	arrange
convince	advise	construct	adapt	advocate
convey	conduct	coordinate	coach	assist
consult	consolidate	delegate	conceptualise	collaborate
communicate	develop	determine	develop	contribute
clarify	evaluate	execute	direct	enlist
detail	explore	maintain	encourage	incorporate
elicit	examine	outline	enforce	partake
explain	facilitate	plan	empower	participate
express	guide	prepare	enable	support
interact	illustrate	prioritise	enhance	
interpret	instill	process	establish	
negotiate	retrieve	propose	identify	
persuade	stimulate	restore	initiate	
present	train	resolve	manage	
	tutor	standardise	motivate	
	verify	suggest	pioneer	
			spearhead	

What if you don't know the answer?

There are situations where you might draw a blank or you just simply don't know the answer. First tip, try buying time by stating the 'S-situation' and 'T-task' bit (the answer is already in the case scenario on that piece of paper in front of you in the interview room). Buying time allows you to re-group and re-organise your thoughts.

You can be honest about it and say:

- 'I am afraid this is something that is slightly beyond my capability/experience.'

Your get-out clause will be

- 'I would escalate this matter to the appropriate seniors.'
- 'I would seek advice from the senior consultant/head of department as to how best to handle this matter.'

Although weak-sounding, this at least demonstrates that you are safe and will seek help if needed.

If the interview question relates to factual contents which you are not familiar with, you could also say 'I would have to do a detailed literature search and read up on the topic before advising the patient further on the matter.'

What if you run out of things to say?

If you run out of things to say before time is up, don't panic. It may be that you have answered well and sailed through the points. However, it is always useful to look back and think back to ensure that you have covered all bases.

A sleek way to review your answer is to provide a short summary of your answer.

- 'To summarise, this is a scenario about … the key issues are … my strategies include …'

Or you can buy time and say honestly:

- 'I am just thinking about my answer and making sure that I have covered all bases.'

Then, if you realise you want to expand on your points:

- 'Pertaining to this strategy, I would like to elaborate further …'
- 'Coming back to this point …'

If you are really out of things to say and feel that you have stated and summarised all your points, politely let the interviewer know that is all you have to say and ask them whether they have more questions for you.

Interview Questions

Below are some sample interview questions and a demonstration of how I would answer them. Be mindful that there is no absolute 'right answer' and that there is no need to memorise answers.

Rather, this is to give you a taste of the sort of interview questions which can be asked and to illustrate the framework of answering.

1) **A senior consultant is leading the ward round and requests a treatment which you know could potentially harm the patient. What do you do?**

- **Situation/issues**: This is a clinical scenario about where patient safety could be jeopardised. In addition, it is a scenario about potential difficult communication with senior colleagues.

- **Task/aim**: Ultimate priority would be to ensure patient safety, while trying to communicate my concerns regarding this potentially harmful treatment effectively with the senior consultant, without confrontation.

- This is in keeping with the ethics principle of 'non-maleficence', in which we should first do no harm to patients.

- However, it is also possible that the consultant in question is much more experienced, and may have his or her rationale for prescribing the treatment. For instance, he or she may be aware of certain clinical guidelines or novel treatment which you might not know of. (This demonstrates insight into your own level of experience, and also demonstrates an ability to view the matter from a different perspective.)

- **Action**: If I definitely know this treatment is going to harm the patient based on solid evidence and recent guidelines, I would ask humbly and in a 'seeking to be taught' manner: 'Pardon me if I am wrong Dr. A. I am slightly concerned that this treatment could cause harm, is there any particular reason to use this treatment or would it be safer to consider other forms of treatment?'

- This conversation should be done in a non-confrontational and a discrete manner (not in front of patient/family).

- **(Rationale)**: It would be best if the conversation isn't confrontational because you want to avoid challenging or embarrassing the consultant, which would lead to a communication breakdown, which will ultimately hamper patient care.

- What if the consultant turns around and says I have been doing this for 20 years, this is my expert opinion? This becomes a slightly difficult situation. However, given the discrepancy in experience and knowledge, it is understandable that the consultant does not want to listen to a MO's opinion. So in this situation, perhaps it is best for the suggestion to come from a fellow senior consultant.

- I would raise my concerns with another senior consultant and discuss this case discretely with him or her. I would seek advice on how best to handle the matter and request to see if it is possible for him/her to help manage the situation.

- I understand that it is not ideal to go behind someone's back and to tell on the person. However, as I mentioned earlier, the utmost priority here is the patient's safety. And I would also ensure that the whole matter is handled discretely.

- **Results/review**: If the consultant is still insistent that I give the treatment, I would apologise and tell him that I'm not able to do it as I'm worried about the possible harm that it would do to the patient.

2) **You are the registrar running clinic. You are running late because there was a cancer patient earlier who needed to be counselled for a major operation. Discussion with that patient took up one hour. It is now 4.45pm. There are still 10 patients waiting to be seen, there is no way that you can finish seeing the patient and the nurses finish at 5pm. What do you do?**

- **Situation**: This is a clinical scenario where an unexpected situation caused a delay in the clinic. It will require prioritisation, delegation and effective communication with staff and patients.

- **(Task/aim)**: To ensure that the patients that require urgent review be seen on that day, and the rest of the patients are managed and informed adequately so to avoid unhappiness and complaints.

- **Action:** Delegation: I would ask the nurse to phone to other doctors in the department to see if anyone is available to help. I would also ask Sister in charge to see if she would be able to arrange for some nurses/assistants to do a short period of overtime, say until 5.30 or 6pm so we could see a few more patients and clear the backlog.

- **Prioritisation:** I would triage the notes, and find out which patients definitely need to be seen today, e.g. cancer patients, patients who are unwell.

- **Communication:** I would then inform the rest of the patients that unfortunately our clinic is overrun (explain why) and it will not be able to see all patients today; all patients who think that they can wait a few days and prefer not to wait, to please go to counter and we will arrange the next available appointment for them. I would extend my apologies for running late and thank them for their understanding and cooperation.

- **Results/review:** After the clinic session, I would sit down and discuss with clinic staff, examine the reason for the overrun and brainstorm to see if there are any areas that we could improve on (Was the clinic overbooked? Should there be more time allotted for cancer patients, e.g. book double slots? Was there enough manpower? Was I being too slow? Were there any other avenues which might have caused the delay in patients being seen, e.g. long registration time, poor clinic workflow), then try and provide a strategy to improve the current workflow so as to avoid similar occurrences in the future.

3) **Patient's family asked you not to tell the patient about his cancer diagnosis. They are telling you to proceed with whatever treatment needed and the family will sign the consent on the patient's behalf. What do you do?**

- **Situation**: First, it is important to recognise this is a difficult clinical situation, especially given the Asian culture where family members play a huge role in the care and decision making for patients. However, to hide the diagnosis from the patient is a violation of patient's autonomy.

- While I respect the patient's family's kind intention in protecting the patient from the painful truth and potential emotional distress, our ultimate responsibility is towards the patient, and the patient has a right to know and to make their own decision, as per the ethics principle of autonomy.

- **Task/aim:** Main aim in this scenario is to do the right thing — which is to break the news of the diagnosis to the patient whilst at the same time convince the family that it is the right thing to do.

- **Action:** I would first explore the family members' concerns and spend time listening to their viewpoint. They may have reasons for making such a request. Often family members are worried about patient's ability to accept the diagnosis. I would extend my sympathy and acknowledge that it is a difficult situation for them.

- (**Rationale**): However, I would also explain to the family the rationale and need for patient to know. In the first instance, patient has the right to know and to be actively involved in decision-making in his or her investigation or treatment process. Furthermore, it would be difficult to initiate further management/treatment without the patient being aware of the diagnosis, and it risks creating confusion, distrust, and communication problems. For instance, if a patient has a laryngeal cancer and may need laryngectomy and end tracheostomy — this is a major operation with various implications (post-op voice loss, potential complications, need for tracheostomy care, etc.) — without the patient knowing the diagnosis, it is difficult for a decision to be made. Imagine the patient not knowing the diagnosis and waking up after a procedure with voice loss and a new breathing hole — it would be most shocking and unpleasant for the patient.

- In certain instances, it also allows the patient to make necessary arrangements for the future.

- In addition, we could also suggest referral to a medical social worker, support group, or palliative medicine team (if warranted), who can aid in supporting the patient and family in the acceptance of diagnosis, as well as emotional support in the treatment journey.

- I would emphasise that we are sympathetic towards the family's plight but reinforce that it is important and essential for the patient to be aware of the diagnosis.

- **Results/review**: If family members still find it difficult to come to agreement, another option would be to allow the family members some time to discuss things among themselves and to relay the news/diagnosis to the patient themselves (with our help). Some families find this more comforting for the patient if acceptable for both the patient and the family.

- We could also be accommodative in allowing a slight delay for the family to try and ease the patient into the diagnosis (but without delaying any crucial treatments). Sometimes what they might need is time to digest the news and come to terms with it.

- However, I would always reassure the family. If it is difficult for the family to break the news to the patient, we are always available to help.

- In addition, we could also suggest referral to a medical social worker, support group, or palliative medicine team (if warranted), who can aid in supporting the patient and family in the acceptance of diagnosis, as well as emotional support in the treatment journey.

4) **At a meeting, your consultant took all the credit for the project that you have done together. You have done the majority of the work and your consultant took a supervisory role. What would you do?**

- **Situation:** This is an ethical situation, whereby the colleague fails to acknowledge efforts for the work done by other colleagues. It is a difficult situation to be in because poor handling of the situation can lead to breakdown of work relationship and can jeopardise future efforts.

- **Task/aim**: Main aim is to avoid being confrontational or causing embarrassment to your consultant/creating an awkward situation, whilst still obtaining the credit that you and your team deserve.

  One should also take into consideration that the above act may be non-intentional. Perhaps in the heat of discussion, the consultant might have forgotten to mention or give credit to you and your team for the work done.

- **Action:** There are a few ways of handling this. If the meeting environment is not the most conducive or appropriate for you to speak up, you could speak to your consultant discretely after to raise your concerns regarding acknowledgement of work done. If the consultant is amenable, you could explore other avenues to obtain credit for your team, such as finding other conferences for you and your team to present the research, or provide authorship for you and your team in the paper publication.

Speaking up during the meeting to seek acknowledge-ment can appear charging and confrontational and may not reflect well on your team and your consultant. However, if the situation allows, you could voice out and thank the consultant for his or her guidance in the project that we have done together. You could acknowledge that whilst your team have worked very hard on this project, without his guidance, the project may not have been completed.

5) **A patient comes in at 2am at night with appendicitis compli-cated with perforation. There is an aortic aneurysm going on in emergency theatre. What would you do?**

- **Situation**: This is a situation that requires accurate assess-ment of the urgency of the situation, prioritisation, as well as organisation of resources to ensure that the patient receives adequate treatment.
- **Task**: Main aim is to ensure the patient receives timely and appropriate treatment.

- **Action**: Hence, I would first assess the patient, taking a good history and performing a thorough examination.

- I would focus on assessing them for any signs of sepsis — e.g. look at the temperature, blood pressure (is the patient in septic shock), heart rate.

- If the patient is toxic or shows any signs of haemodynamic instability, this would be an indication for the patient to undergo surgery more urgently. This is to remove the source of sepsis.

- I would send off some basic investigations in preparation for surgery. This includes sending off bloods including full blood count, renal panel, GXM, do ECG, CXR and check the time of the patient's last meal/drink.

- In addition, I would institute some basic management, including getting IV access, starting antibiotics and IV fluid.

- I would inform my senior (registrar/consultant) about the patient and report to them my clinical findings. I would also make them aware of the potential delay for surgery owing to another emergency surgery.

- I would send in an OT chit to book the patient on the emergency theatre and inform the anaesthetist. If the patient is very septic, I would consult my seniors and consider booking a high-dependency bed.

- I would find out how long more the aortic aneurysm surgery is going to take. I would then liaise with the anaesthetic team to see whether it is possible to set up another theatre if the aneursym surgery is going to be long. I would also explain the rationale behind the urgency.

- **Review/results**: If it is not possible to set up another theatre and the aortic aneurysm surgery is going to be long, other options include first stabilising and optimising the patient with IV antibiotics, IV fluids and inotropes until theatre slot is available, or to consider transferring the patient to another hospital if absolutely required. I will make sure the patient is monitored and regularly reviewed, and any deterioration to be informed to the registrar.

- At all times, I would keep the patient and family up to date about the situation.

6) **You are one of the senior associates/partners in a General Practice group. Your boss asks your opinion about promotion of one of the two other junior partners to senior partner. He intends to promote GP A, who is thin, rather than GP B, who is fat. He tells you that it would be better for the image of the group and would provide better confidence for patients in management of patient health.**

- **Situation**: This is a potential situation of workplace discrimination based on one's looks and weight.

- **Task/aim:** This requires careful and fair review to ensure that the there is no workplace discrimination regardless of size/sex/age/preferences, yet taking into account the need for a corporate group (GP group) to maintain its stance in health promotion.

- **Action:** My view is that a person should not be discriminated against based on their looks or weight. I think in consideration for work promotion, one should focus mainly on the partner's work capabilities, but also taking into account of the partner's ability to work well in a team and their contribution to the group.

- I would urge the boss to review and compare the candidates objectively prior to making the decision. This can be done by reviewing their clinical work, obtaining patient and colleague feedback, reviewing figures/statistics, e.g. number of patient seen, number of complaints/compliments, involvement in work activities and so on.

- **Review/results:** However, I am also aware that one of the main responsibilities of GP is health promotion. Often, in this setting, doctors are also double as role models when delivering patient education.

- So it is not unreasonable for GP to maintain a healthy image so as to be more consistent, effective and convincing when advising patient on health issues. Although this shouldn't be a the deciding factor in consideration in the work promotion, perhaps it would not be unreasonable for the boss or other senior partner to speak to GPB privately to advise him/her on this matter.

7) **An angry patient comes in with nasal fracture one month after the event due to ED wrong booking/clinic staff miscommunication. What do you do?**

   - **Situation:** In this situation, miscommunication has led to suboptimal treatment of a patient. The patient could have qualified for a manipulation of nasal fracture, which is a simple procedure but needed to be done within a window of two to three weeks after initial injury. Beyond that period, the nasal bone is fused in the new fracture position.

- As a result of the delayed appointment, should the patient require surgery, he will have to undergo a much bigger procedure in the form of septorhinoplasty, which can carry higher risks, e.g. septal perforation, numbness of incisors, scarring, etc.

- Mistakes like these affect patient outcome and risk creating unhappiness and mistrust from patients.

- **Task**: Main aim is to ensure the patient receives appropriate treatment and to achieve the optimal outcome. In addition, the appointment booking process needs to be reviewed in order to prevent such mistakes in the future.

- **Action**: I would first spend some time listening to the patient's complaint. He or she might have a lot of frustration and concerns that they want to express. By listening to what they have to say, it allows me to pinpoint their main concerns and helps me address them.

- In addition, it helps the patient feel that we value their opinion and that we do take the matter seriously.

- I would extend my apologies over the situation and reassure him that this was unintentional and we will definitely look into what went wrong and how we can improve the booking system.

- I would offer to perform an assessment on his condition, asking if he noticed any new onset of blocked nose since the injury and if he has noticed any change in the shape of his nose. Not all nasal fractures require fixing as some nasal fractures are not displaced and therefore can be managed conservatively.

- I would discuss my assessment findings with the patient and lay out the treatment options for the patient. Again, these discussions show respect for the patient's autonomy and are useful for formation of partnership in the management of patient's health.

- **Review/results**: I would then allow the patient some time to think through the options before deciding. If the patient is still unhappy about the treatment process, I would offer to help patient obtain a second opinion. If the patient wants to make a complaint, I would provide clear instructions or have an assistant accompany him to patient relation service to lodge a complaint. I would again extend my apologies for the inconvenience caused.

  In addition, I would also perform a review of this patient's appointment booking process to identify the problem in this case. I would then discuss the matter with my department to make an effort to rectify/improve the process.

8) **Fellow MO is becoming dishevelled and withdrawn. He is acting eccentrically, with outbursts of anger against clinic staff. What do you do? Who should be involved?**

   - **Situation/issues:** This is a scenario where the emotional health of a colleague and his ability to maintain professional conduct is of concern. These can affect his work performance and can therefore impact patient safety. There are likely to be some reasons behind the onset of this new behaviour. It may be that he is suffering from certain psychological/physical health problems or that he might be going through some stressful life events such as bereavement, debt and family conflicts. There may also be a possibility of burnout from work.

   - **Task:** What would be helpful in this case is to provide help to the colleague in question in a discrete and non-intrusive manner, in order to prevent any downward spiral which may affect patient care and his career. It is important to make him aware that help and resources are available.

- **Action:** First, I would have to decide how to approach the colleague in question. If we are close and have reasonable rapport, I would try and approach him in a discrete manner. However, if he happens to be a colleague with whom I do not have close contact, he may find it intrusive and uncomfortable for me to ask about his personal problems. Hence, it may be best that help comes from someone whom he trusts and someone who has the ability to help, such as his tutor/supervisor.

- If I could talk to this colleague, I would first let him know that we are worried about his current condition and explain that the recent incidents as mentioned have triggered concerns that it might affect his work performance. I would ask him if he is aware of such problems.

- I would offer a listening ear and help him explore his concerns. I would let him know that sometimes it is easier to talk about the problems rather than letting the stress accumulate. Hopefully I can also offer a fresh or different perspective to his problems. This could help in stress reduction and hopefully enable him to have a sense of better control.

- I would let him know that, like everyone else, doctors are equally vulnerable to sickness. There are cultural/professional barriers that view this sort of psychological/physical illness as personal weakness. However, denial of the problem does not help. The cumulative effect of emotional exhaustion is detrimental to his work, as it would often lead to detachment and reduced capacity to empathise with patients. Ultimately this can affect patient care and his career. There is no shame in seeking help when it is needed, and it is particularly important for it to be done before it is too late.

- If he is not comfortable talking about his problem, I would ask him what I can do to help — perhaps I could take on some of his calls or duties (only if he wants me to) to allow him some respite from work or time to deal with these problems.

- I would also let him know about other resources for help such as his supervisor, psychological medicine within the hospital, financial advisors for doctors and so on. I would reassure him that all this would be done in a confidential manner to respect his privacy and to avoid stigmatisation.

- **Review/results**: Hopefully the colleague is amenable to being helped. However, if he is not and continues to deteriorate, continual probing from me might lead to breach of confidence and breakdown in our work relationship. In addition, given my position as a junior doctor, it may be difficult and ineffective for me to handle such matters.

- I would raise my concerns discretely with his supervisor/ tutor, who may be more apt in handling the matter.

Interview Preparation

1) Before the interview

- **Mock interviews:** Try and practice some interview questions with your colleagues. Try and look up past year questions and use them as a guide. Practice talking through scenario and video record yourself if you can. You will notice things and habits which you may not have noticed before. I used to say a lot of 'um, ah, er...' and used too many hand gestures during the practice sessions. You may also notice sentences which you might want to construct in a different way.

- **Read around**: It is useful to read around certain common topics and guidelines — such as Gillick competence, the

SMC ethical code and ethical guidelines, clinical practice guidelines and so on. It will demonstrate to your interviewers that you keep abreast of recent developments and helps strengthen your arguments.

2) **Day of interview**

- **Dress to kill:** Always good to overdress than under. You won't get extra points for dressing well, but you certainly don't want to stand out for the wrong reasons. First impressions matter. For guys — minimum of a well-pressed shirt and tie, ideally with a suit. For ladies — minimum of a well-pressed blouse with formal skirt/slacks or pant/skirt suit. Failure to dress appropriately shows a lack of respect of the event, lack of interview experience and lack of research.

- **Arrive early:** Account for the time needed to look for the venue and time needed to regain your composure and thoughts.

- Put your phone on 'silent'.

In Summary

The interview is an important part of the selection process. My final advice to you: Be aware of the process and requirements, practice and prepare extensively and keep calm on the day itself. Good luck!

8

EQ and Etiquette — Make the Best of a Rotation!

"I've learned that people will forget what you said, people will forget what you did, but people will never forget how you made them feel."
— Maya Angelou

> ## Key Points
>
> - Emotional quotient or emotional intelligence is the ability to identify and manage our own, as well as others' emotion.
> - It consists of a few components, including self-awareness, self-regulation, social awareness, social skills and self-motivation.
> - Higher emotional intelligence is associated with better doctor-patient relationship, increased empathy, better

> teamwork and communication skills and more effective stress management.
> - Etiquette is a code of behaviour/practice that is socially acceptable in a particular setting. Most of these etiquettes exist in order to ensure the smooth-running of the clinical work.
> - When rotating through a department as an elective student or junior doctor, in addition to being clinically competent, having good EQ and maintaining good etiquette can help you foster a favourable impression, which can impact your evaluation and entry into the Residency training.

Whilst writing this book, I had a chat with one of the newly recruited residents on how she got into Residency. I knew her as a student rotating through our department. Of the students I have met, she is by far the most exemplary when it comes to career navigation. To give you an idea, she was successful in her first Residency application attempt, straight out of medical school. Not an easy feat for a medical student. By the time of her Residency application, she was well-known and well-liked by staff at all three institutions in the Specialty she was applying for. She maximised her opportunities with well-planned electives, obtained first author publications in high impact factor journals (all as a student), as well as ensured attendance at most relevant local and regional courses and conferences. This was in addition to having sound knowledge and great aptitude.

Hence, when I asked, what she thought to be the (other) important factors leading to successful Residency application (in addition to well-planned electives/rotation and research projects), it was interesting that she remarked that having the **'right EQ'** is important. I am inclined to agree. We spoke about it for a while. The term was used very loosely to mean how you carry yourself and how you respond in different situations in the workplace to help leave a favourable impression on your potential selectors. I divided this further into two components — **EQ and Etiquette**.

What is EQ?

EQ — Emotional quotient or emotional intelligence is the ability to identify and manage our own, as well as others' emotions (Mayer *et al.*, 1997). It is this ability to understand oneself and have awareness of the impact of your actions on others that guides you and helps you navigate day-to-day challenges. It consists of a few components:

- **Self-awareness:** Ability to recognise your own emotions and what their effect is on others.
- **Self-regulation:** Ability to manage and control your own emotions.
- **Social awareness:** Being aware and showing empathy for others (e.g. patients/colleagues) emotions and concerns, taking into account the situation and their needs in your actions.
- **Social skills**: Ability to interact and communicate effectively.
- **Self-motivation:** Ability to promote self-growth to achieve in one's life.

Why is EQ important?

Medical school entry is fiercely competitive. By this mechanism of selection, there is no lack of high IQ doctors at the end of the production line. Except that, in real practice, having a high IQ does not necessarily equate to success. Rather, many studies have shown that EQ is an essential component in successful practice.

The modern day doctor requires not just sound clinical ability, but also the ability to connect and respond to patient's emotions and needs in order to deliver effective patient-centred care. In a systematic review of emotional intelligence in medicine by Arora *et al.*, 16 articles which were included in the review showed that higher emotional intelligence is associated with better doctor-patient relationship, increased empathy, better teamwork and communication skills, more effective stress management, organisational commitment, as well as leadership (Arora *et al.*, 2010).

Emotional intelligence has also been shown to have a significant relationship with patient satisfaction (Azimi *et al.*, 2010). Dugan *et al.* also showed improved patient satisfaction scores were seen in a group of residents and faculty after Emotional Intelligence training (Dugan *et al.*, 2014).

Residency training comes with its own set of challenges and stressors. This includes

— The need to understand patient's perspective, address patients' need for information and reassurance, as well as to promote doctor-patient relationship
— The need to maintain collegial relationship with colleagues in order to create a collaborative, supportive, interdependent network
— The need to position oneself as a receptive and responsive learner
— The need to take on other roles eg. leadership and managerial roles.
— The need to demonstrate various aptitudes eg. team working and organisational skills
— The need to amass and assimilate large amount of knowledge whilst maintaining work-life balance

Hence, EQ has become an essential component in patient care. EQ helps you tune into and respond to patients' concerns, thus optimising clinical outcomes and patient satisfaction. It can help you deal with difficult clinical situations patients in denial or unhappy patients/family members. One of the most effective ways to learn, I find, is to see someone good, handling a difficult situation. Another way is to see a variety of people do it, learn the keywords that they used, or the key disarming/defusing points and try and apply it the next time.

EQ extends beyond patient encounters. It also has impact on your interaction with your peers, juniors, seniors, nursing staff, allied health specialist and administrative staff. It is essential for effective functioning at the work place. Doctors can be egoistical and can have the tendency to impose their expectations or view-points on others. This can sometimes lead to hurt feelings or an unpleasant work environment. Possessing some emotional intelli-gence can help you communicate your perspective and expecta-tions in a team setting in a diplomatic manner, ensuring you achieve what you need yet avoiding unhappiness within the team. In this aspect, I find that it is often about aligning agendas from both parties, with a little bit of compromise in between.

EQ helps you get along with your peers and handling people who are difficult to get along with. To be a successful resident, one has to give and take. People are often motivated by self-interests. Conflict can arise when the same individuals have a very strong sense of personal entitlement. Unpleasant situations may arise as a result — for example, operating time, weekend calls, and so on. So, the senior resident in charge usually needs some level of EQ to nagivate these potentially inflammatory circumstances.

On a personal level, having a high EQ can help doctors regu-late their emotions and hence increase their ability to cope with stress. To be a successful resident and doctor, you need to build resilience in the face of adversity. This can come in the form of criticism, unfulfilled expectations, unfulfilled ambitions and out-right hostility sometimes. One needs EQ to manage yourself and others. It can be useful to take a step back, reflect and consider the larger perspective, rather than react in haste and land your-self in an unfavourable position. I personally find discussing the situation with close friends within the field or mentors helpful. They often help you see a different aspect of things. In addition, the collective wisdom of your friends/mentor can help provide more strategies to deal with the situation. The caveat here is to speak to those within the field but perhaps with no direct conflict of interest.

That said, this is a subject of contention. Some of the most brilliant surgeons I know haven't got the best EQ, yet have stellar reputation and careers. However, times are changing. Patient in this day and age may demand more than the paternalistic interactions from doctors. Similarly, there is more and more emphasis on teamwork rather than individualism. Therefore, having the good EQ can always come in handy in maintaining good workplace and doctor-patient relationships.

Application of EQ in the Clinical Setting

1) The angry patient

This is one example on social awareness, of how to defuse a difficult situation that I learned from my seniors. For instance, it is a common encounter for most of us to have patients come into the consult room to complain of long wait times. What I found useful to do as the patient enter the room is to:

a)   Be earnest and empathetic in apologizing about the long wait.

b)   Ask the patients what time they arrived. (I find this to be the key point in defusing the emotionally charged patients, which is simply to acknowledge the situation. Whilst asking the question is completely irrelevant to the actual medical consult, the additional minute in doing this usually puts you on their side, in that they would feel that you are seeing things from their perspective, and this will usually make the subsequent consult smoother. Through the years, this has worked very well for me. Sometimes I throw in a 'was it difficult to get parked?', nothing builds rapport like it. Heh.

c) I usually then follow up with a "Oh that is a very long wait. Let's see how we can help you make up for it. Tell me about what brings you here today ..."

I guess we could argue all day here about why one should apologise when the long wait is not entirely your fault. However, I'd like to think of it as extending a little empathy in apologising for the situation that neither you nor the patient has asked for. You see, whilst you have your reasons for running late in the consult, e.g. ward rounds took too long so you started your clinic late, or that there was a cancer patient who needed more consult time; the patients too, have their reasons to be angry or annoyed. For instance, some patients may have to rush to pick their kids up from school after the clinic consult, or some are care givers who have to bring the patient with chronic conditions for multiple appoint-ments in addition to dealing with financial difficulties from medical bills and may well be burnt out from caregiver stress.

Whilst we can't solve every single problem, a little acknowledg-ment of the situation goes a long way. You immediately recruit the patient/carer to your side. Sure, they might still vent a bit, but most of the times you will find the patients become more agreeable. Patients are often more forgiving and understanding than you think. They understand well that often it is not our intention to make them wait and they do know that most times, not much can be done about it. Hence, from our end, a little awareness of how these patients might feel and the pressures they face, a little empathy, shown in a form of acknowledgment, often helps.

2) The lazy colleague

This is a situation on self-regulation and application of social skills. It is a common occurrence that junior doctors squabble over roster and/or clinical responsibilities. It is easy to get angry over a col-league who is not pulling his/her weight in sharing out the clinical duties. However, being angry and yelling harsh words or snarky remarks at your colleague often aggravates the situation and does not solve anything. So, it would be a demonstration of good EQ if you could self-regulate your own emotions, control your anger and look for solutions.

A good demonstration of social skills is to find creative ways in communicating your needs/agenda across. For instance, in this situation, it is easy to be accusatory and criticise your colleague for not doing his/her share. Instead, you could try re-packaging your words. Instead of demanding that your colleague do his/her share of work:

"Everyone is taking on more calls, you should stop being lazy and do 5 calls too!."

You could re-script it to a "**I need you help in this**" sort of phrasing:

"There are a few people sitting for exams soon, we hope to help cover their on-calls so they can focus on their exams. So, our department is really tight in manpower this month. Could you help out by taking one extra call? It would really be helpful for our team. When the rest are back from exams, they will do make-up calls."

This approach also explains the 'why' (to help out colleagues who are sitting for exams), which helps reason and resonate better with the other party whom you are negotiating with, which helps increase the chances of aligning agendas from both sides.

What is Etiquette?

Etiquette is a code of behaviour/practice that is socially acceptable in a particular setting. Most people relate etiquette to supercilious, exclusive high-society practices which are both dreary and snobbish. However, the truth is far from that.

In the healthcare setting, be it ward, clinic or in the operating theatre, there are often some unwritten rules or expectations on how you should carry yourself. These are often long-existing and relate to the differing roles that each healthcare professional is expected to play. Most of these 'rules' exist in order to ensure the smooth running of clinical work.

For instance, when a nurse is dispensing medication, it is best not to disturb him/her so as to avoid medication error. When in the operating theatre, students/nurses/doctors/drug reps are expected to wear different colour theatre caps so as to make it easy for others to recognise their role and ensure appropriate delegation of jobs.

Why is Etiquette Important?

Using proper etiquette is a demonstration of your respect for the setting which you have been given the privilege to be a part of. It affects how people in the setting (senior doctors, nurses, allied health, patients, work colleagues) view you. It reflects on your situational awareness and whether you are considerate enough to act in a manner that makes it convenient for others. Not the least it makes people comfortable in your presence.

EQ and Etiquette — Making the Best of a Rotation

When rotating through a department as an elective student or junior doctor, competency aside, the impression which you leave on your consultant/team matters. It matters whether you appear considerate, engaging and diligent, and that you work as a team player. The initial impression that the team forms of you can impact your evaluation. Not the least it can lead to more opportunities for learning, research experience and good references for your Residency application.

The tips below are a collation of experiences — some personal, some from colleagues and others from seniors. These are just for your reference, really. Nobody is perfect. Nobody can be that perfect. I can't say that I am always 100% compliant wither. However, it helps to be aware, and know that we are all works in progress.

1) Introduce yourself and state your intent

- Students come and go. Most clinicians are perhaps not that most aware of the clinical rotation schedules. But usually, we will come to notice two to three new faces in white coats tailing us quietly during rounds, trying hard not to get into the way, but eagerly (still quietly) observing.

- Most of them (you) don't say anything until and unless approached by one of the team members in our rounds — behaviour which I find peculiar.

- I think it is important, or at least it is basic courtesy, to introduce yourself to the most senior person leading the round/in the operating theatre (e.g. the main surgeon) and to ask if you can follow/observe/partake in the rounds/surgery/sit in for clinic.

- I feel the onus is upon you to try and build this rapport between you and the team that you are attached to. Sometimes, some of the team members in the team may be friendly or kind enough to ask you who you are and introduce you to the rest of the team, but that really depends on your luck.

- If you stand silently and follow silently during the ward round, chances are, ward rounds being so business-like, nobody will notice you or say anything to you or teach you anything.

- But if you introduce yourself, that makes it easier for you to ask questions about the patients/cases later. It also makes it easier for the team to interact with you if they know who you are and what you are there for.

- Obviously, it is important to find the right moment — not when the consultant is breaking bad news to the patient and not when the consultant is at a critical step in the operation. Do it in between patients, do it as you are walking from one ward to another, do it at the beginning of the day before the start of operation, etc.

- State your name, your year, what you are there for and whether you're interested in the specialty (always helps!).

2) Presenting/referring etiquette

- As a final-year medical student/junior doctor, it is likely that you have to present patients during rounds or meetings and refer blue letters to other specialties.

- Being concise and clear helps you get the information across effectively, not to mention leaving a good impression on your bosses and the people you work with.

- Start by introducing yourself and which team you are from or who you are calling on behalf of, e.g. 'My name is Chu Qin, ENT Medical Officer calling on behalf of Dr. Mok.'

- Give a **'heading'** for the story that you are about to tell. E.g.

  o 'I am referring a patient with ST elevation myocardial infarction for consideration of percutaneous coronary intervention.'

  o 'I would like to refer a patient with asthma for optimisation of her medical therapy prior to surgery.'

  o Essentially you are stating the patient's problem and what you want the other person to do in one sentence.

  Rather than

  o 'I would like to discuss a patient name XXX, IC number XXX, under the care of consultant XXX. She is currently admitted with four days history of SOB and cough, but also has back pain and haematuria....'

  o You not wrong in stating all the details, except that people usually don't have such a long attention span. If you give them the 'heading' first, it quickly highlights the objective of your call and helps them pick up the important information in the subsequent lines that you are about to say.

- After stating the heading, you can then go on to illustrate your case by painting a **relevant background history**.

  o 'This is a 56-year-old male, smoker and drinker, with a background of ischaemic heart disease s/p coronary artery bypass grafting, hypertension and diabetes presented with one day history of chest pain radiating to his left arm, associated with...'

  o 'This is a 60-year-old male who is on dual antiplatelet for a recent stroke presented with two days history of haematemesis.'

  o Giving relevant history helps **paint a picture** of the patient, which would help the person on the other end of the call/your consultant gauge the severity/urgency of the problem.

  o Most of all, it shows that you have given thought as to what the causal mechanism is and that you are aware of its relevance to the patient's presentation.

- The rest of the history should include:
  o Any relevant investigations
  o Any basic management performed

- For referrals, end your referral with 'would really appreciate your help with (what you want the person to do)':

  o 'We would really appreciate your help in reviewing this patient for consideration of intubation and ICU care.'

- For presentation during rounds, end your presentation with a one or two sentence short summary:

  o '**In summary,** this is a 24-year-old patient with epiglottitis who is now stable after a treatment with dexamethasone and is now being monitored in the high-dependency ward.'

3) Theatre etiquette

- Introduce yourself and ask the most senior person in the OT (make sure you ask the correct team — surgeon vs anaesthetist vs charge nurse) for permission to join him/her.

- Be there on time.

- You can sometimes ask to scrub; I find it helpful as a student or junior doctor when I scrubbed. It gives you the proximity to have a better view and if you are lucky, you might get to do a thing or two, e.g. suturing, wound closure. However, don't get upset if you get turned down. The surgeons often have other considerations if they say no to you.

- If you can, try and look up the theatre list the day before so that you can read up and have some basic understanding of the case/surgery.

- Ask for permission to read through the patient's notes so that you at least understand the background history, indication for surgery and relevant investigations, e.g. audiogram for ear surgery.

- Maintain sterility — avoid touching the sterile drapes and instruments. If you are unclear, the scrub nurse or OT nurses can usually give you guidance.

- Be helpful without getting in the way. There are always things to do if you are not scrubbed. E.g. help tie the surgeon's gown, scroll through scans for the surgeon, help transfer the patient if you can, adjust the OT lights if you know how to.

- Obviously, you are not there to be a thambi. You don't have to bend over backwards to do everything. You are there to learn. Learning takes precedence over trying to please others. However, if there are simple things which you can help with without hindering your learning, why not? At the very least, it will make the surgical team feel like you are part of the team, which can aid in your subsequent learning.

- If you are not sure of what to do, don't rush into it. Most students aren't sure what is appropriate for them to do. First observe and learn. Offer to help, ask if they (the team) would like you to do certain things, e.g. 'Can I help you with this gown?' 'Would you like me to help answer your phone?'

- Ask questions if you want, but pick the right time and right person.

- Don't piss off the OT scrub nurses. If it means putting on the correct coloured scrub hat or registering at the main reception counter — do it.

If you are the junior doctor in the OT, some initiative should be taken to:

- Pull up the relevant scans (X-ray, CT, MRI) on the computer before the start of operation.

- If possible, fill up the investigation forms before operation starts, e.g. histology forms, or frozen section forms (scrub nurses will love you for that).

- If you are aware of any special equipment/instrument that is required for the operation, or any certain preferences of the consultant surgeon, you could help communicate this to the scrub nurses and have them on standby. But avoid being too brash or presumptuous — you can make a suggestion if you are certain. But leave it to the nurses ultimately, because sometimes, the nurses know better than you do.

- Make sure you sort out the necessary paper work, e.g. prescription, MC, operation notes, any audit forms.

- Ask to scrub in when you can. For one, you get to go closer and see better of what's going on during the operation, not the least, occasionally you might get to do something when the opportunity arises e.g. close some simple wounds. But don't get too upset if you get turned down. Do understand the team's priority is still maintaining the patient and team's safety, including yours. Sometimes it may be too crowded for another person to scrub in; you need to respect that decision. However, do know that you will always get more chances next time.

- When assisting in an operation, don't get in the way, don't block the OT light. Try and gauge the surgeon's preferences — some surgeons would like you to have initiative and do things without being asked. But some surgeons prefer that you don't move unless instructed.

- Do remember to see your own post-operative patients, particularly if you have done the operation. It shows a sense of ownership and reliability. It demonstrates to your seniors that you are able to follow through.

4) Be open to ideas — Listen and learn

- I am going to give you an example — let's say I go into the operating theatre today and I'm operating with a senior consultant. First case is a tonsillectomy — one which most year 1 and 2 ENT residents frequently perform and are usually able to perform independently. So if the senior consultant asks me (as they often do): Do you know how to do it?

- So, if I answer 'Yes, I have done the operation before and I know how to do it', chances are, the consultant will let me carry on and nothing will come of it. I will still be able to complete the operation in the way that I know.

- What if I had said 'Yes, I have done it before, but could you tell me how you usually do it? What is your preference?' It opens up learning opportunities for me. I will then have the chance to learn that consultant's method and add that to my own repertoire.

- Similarly, I had research projects with two students. Both projects were scheduled for presentation at the departmental meeting. I offered to go through their presentations with both students. Student A agreed and we spent hours going through the slides, the flow of the presentation and what to say. Student B declined. While Student B had an uneventful presentation, Student A went on to win a best oral presentation prize at a regional meeting.

- Most people pride themselves on being liberal. So if you tell them you are okay with it, they are not likely to impose and insist that they teach you their method of presentation. They will let you crack on. Hence you might have just lost an opportunity to learn something new.

- My belief is that there is always something you can learn from everyone. Try and be aware of these opportunities for learning and don't turn them down.

5) Show initiative

- Yes, I understand. As a medical student, the first mantra is 'try not to get in the way'. But there is always something to do without getting in the way — help swing the curtains around when the consultant is about to examine a patient, pass some gloves, get tissues for crying family members, if you're in the clinic — open the door for wheelchair-bound patients/or just patients. Get involved!

- Try and have an awareness of what is required to help facilitate things for your team. These are things that will come to you if you make the effort to observe. For instance, as a non-trainee in ENT rounds, I would always carry a pen torch and have some tongue depressors ready — as there was a higher frequency of examining the oral cavity during rounds compared to other specialties. It makes rounds smoother as it saves you and your team from having to scramble to look for a tongue depressor (a rare commodity) in the ward.

6) Position yourself as a great learner

- A large part of learning in medicine is still modeled upon the apprenticeship system, where clinical knowledge and practical skills are imparted from the mentor or teacher to the student in a see-learn-do manner.

- Whether you are a medical student or junior doctor, in the span of your career, it is beneficial to enhance your own teachability, so to secure solid training in your journey to deepen your understanding of medicine

- This involves being responsive, receptive and reciprocative.

  o **Be responsive**
     People respond in accordance to how you relate and react to them. An apathetic student is unlikely to rouse the enthusiasm of the teacher and vice versa.

     As a Resident, I taught different groups of medical students who rotated through our department. I found myself making extra efforts for students who were more enthusiastic and responsive.

     There were a few groups who were constantly inquisitive and curious. These were the students who came back to me after reading some materials with more questions, sometimes challenging my points. It was refreshing. Sensing that they were keen, when I had interesting ward patients, or clinical signs in clinic patients, I would invite them along to show them more cases and do more ad-hoc teachings. Their enthusiasm was simply infectious and encouraged me to teach more. It was pure joy.

     There are various ways to demonstrate your responsiveness, e.g. when asked a question you don't know the answer to, try to look it up and follow up with the answer with your tutor. Actions like these help your tutor know that you have made an effort to learn about the topic.

In addition, after being taught, try and demonstrate that you are able to apply it. This helps demonstrate to your tutor that you paid attention and understood what was taught. Gesture like these are encouraging for tutors (at least it was, for me when I taught) — it is an acknowledgment of that what they taught have sunk in and that they have made an impact, however small it may be.

- **Be receptive**
  When told about your mistakes or how you could improve things, try to be receptive about your tutor's opinions and suggestions. At the very least, acknowledge their opinions. Better yet, if you can, try and demonstrate that you are able to apply in the next sitting. Your willingness to receive and accept suggestions portrays a more amenable and malleable character, which makes others more eager to teach. Regardless of how good you think you might be, it is important to be aware and understand the fact that seniors often have more experience than you and are more likely to be able to help guide you forward in the same field of expertise.

- **Reciprocate**
  A large part of teaching occurs out of goodwill and most tutors do it in their own time. A little gratitude goes a long way. Often, a little thank you, an appreciative feedback or an acknowledgment is all that is needed. These reciprocal actions have a binding capacity that makes various continuing relationship possible.

- Other ways of enhancing your teachability include asking intelligent questions, which requires effort in pre-reading to be able to formulate more critical and relevant questions.

- Other than that, show interest, demonstrate a desire and willingness to learn. Be able to learn, un-learn and re-learn. "It is what you learn after you know it all that matters" — John Wooden

7) Be present

- Be present. Be there long enough so that people will remember you when any opportunity arises, e.g. when setting a cannula, if there's a need for an extra assistant in the OT, when there are interesting cases, etc. There was an elective student whom I met during my GS posting who was always there during rounds (morning and exit), always around helping the house officers with some of the simple jobs and who was always there when we needed an extra pair of hands. Naturally, when the OT needed an extra assistant or when there were interesting cases, consultants and registrars offen remember to ask her to join in.

- Be there when the team needs you. In my TTSH posting, there was a particular medical student who was always there to help retract in quite a few of our long strenuous cancer operations. We still talk about her up till today — mostly because we were grateful for her help, especially because we were short of manpower. Because the team became familiar with her, she got to stitch and close some wounds. As I recall, the team consultant also gave her some research projects to do.

8) Provide solutions

- When given a task, try and see 'solutions' rather than 'problems' in it. Focusing on solutions not only feels more positive, it is also more productive. Rather than seeing problems and difficulties which require effort to overcome, seeing solutions means having the opportunity to create improvements.

- Nobody likes a whiner (note to self). Have a **'can do'** attitude, well, without overpromising or being too cocky.

- E.g.

   o **Problem-focused:** 'This project may not be feasible because there are too few patients', versus

Solution-focused: 'Our department may not have enough patients to achieve an adequate sample size, but we could extend the research to other hospitals to increase our recruitment rate.'

- **Problem-focused:** 'We don't usually refer patients to TBCU (Tuberculosis Control Unit). So I don't know how to do it.'

  Solution-focused: 'I have not referred patients to TBCU before, but I can try and find out from other house officers how to do it.

9) If you are in deep shit, first pour more shit on yourself

- Wise words passed on to me by a Breast Registrar whom I worked with in the UK. When you get into trouble, own up and first pour more shit on yourself. For example,

  - 'This is entirely my fault, I should have made sure this happened...'

  - 'I am really sorry about what happened, I could have done this to make it better...'

- From the seniors' point of view, it demonstrates two things:

  a) You have insight and you are aware of your mistake

  b) You are sorry for your mistake (which reduces the need for them to whack/yell at you)

- All of us make mistakes. But if you are able to acknowledge your mistake, apologise and learn from it, it makes you a safer doctor and a trainable one.

In Summary

I think learning etiquette and developing one's EQ is a lifelong premise. I, for one, cannot claim to be the master of my own EQ or of etiquette. However, being aware of this premise, and the potential effect it can have on one's life and career, is always a good start. For this chapter, I leave you with the quote below:

'Life is like a game of chess. To win you have to make a move. Knowing which move to make comes with insight and knowledge, and by learning the lessons that are accumulated along the way.'
— Allan Rufus

References

1. Mayer JD, Salovey P. (1997) What is emotional intelligence? In: Salovey P, Sluyter DJ, eds. *Emotional Development and Emotional Intelligence: Educational Implications.* New York, NY: Basic Books, pp. 3–31.
2. Arora S, Ashrafian H, Davis R. (2010) Emotional intelligence in medicine: a systematic review through the context of the ACGME competencies. *Med Educ* **44(8):** 749–764.
3. Azimi S, AsgharNejad F AA, Kharazi FMJ, Khoei N. (2010)Emotional intelligence of dental students and patient satisfaction. *Eur J Dent Educ* **14(3):** 129–32.
4. Dugan JW, Weatherly RA, Girod DA, *et al.* (2014) A longitudinal study of emotional intelligence training for otolaryngology residents and faculty. *JAMA Otolaryngol Head Neck Surg* **140(8):** 720–6.
5. Talarico JF, Varon AJ, Banks SE, *et al.* (2013) Emotional intelligence and the relationship to resident performance: a multi-institutional study. *J Clin Anesth* **25(3):** 181–7.

9

What If It Does Not Work Out?

"Everybody is a genius. But if you judge a fish by its ability to climb a tree, it will live its whole life believing that it is stupid."
— Albert Einstein

"Every experience in your life is being orchestrated to teach you something you need to know to move forward." — Brian Tracy

"Do what you can with what you have where you are."
— Theodore Roosevelt

Key Points

- If you did not match, take some time out to review and reassess your standing/position in the Residency application race.
- It is worth sitting down and getting someone (consultants programme director, consultants who are in the interview

panel, current residents/registrars) to critically appraise your CV and your performance. Get the person to point out what is lacking in your repertoire and how you could improve on it.

- Until the next application, it is important to fully utilise the time to reorganise your strategies. Keep working on the items (clinical rotation/research/poster/presentation/organising an event for the department) that can help increase your chance of success in the next round.

- Other options to consider include: application to other specialties with similar traits, being a resident physician or service registrar, other healthcare-related jobs including healthcare administration/management jobs, public health jobs, health consulting, healthcare research, and pharmaceutical work.

Everyone has their relative strengths and weaknesses. The flaw in our education system is that it does have a fixed mould and self-selects the few who fit it. It is a likely reality that the Residency system, or the institution, or the department will have an affinity towards certain personalities. Some people are just more suited towards certain institutions, specialties or departments. Or it may be that some people have more knack in navigating their career than others.

But hey, life isn't all standardised. Neither are your patients or your clinical work. Just because you don't fit the mould or measure up to certain expectations does not necessarily mean you don't have talents of your own. Just because certain institutions are not able to recognise or cultivate your talent doesn't mean you should give up on it too. So, don't beat yourself up for it. Know that you too have particular strengths. You might have to do some introspection and find out what they are. Below are a few things you can do.

1) Review and Reassess

If you did not match, take some time out to review and reassess.

- **How many places are up for grabs? Who is your competition?**
  As mentioned Chapter 2, be realistic without denying yourself the opportunity. If there are very few places and many other applicants queuing in front of you, you might want to consider other options, for instance, application to other institutions or other specialties. Alternatively, if you feel it is a matter of waiting for your turn (e.g. you think you stand a better chance next application), you could continue to work on getting in the next round.

- **Was it your clinical performance?**
  Is there anything in your day to day work in the department which you could improve on? Are there any other avenues for you to showcase your ability and team spirit? Advice can be sought from your supervisor, the registrars or the residents you work with.

- **Was it a CV problem?**
  Did your CV give you the best chance of being successful? If you have the opportunity, have a look at the CV of the successful applicants — what was it that they had that you didn't? Was it the research? Was it relevant work experience?

- **Do the selectors genuinely favour your application?**
  As per one of my senior consultants — some senior doctors find it awkward to say 'no chance' to the applicant even when chances are pretty slim. This can lead to wasted time and effort in rotations and research work. Hence, it is worth finding someone who is involved/familiar with the selection process and whom you can rely on to give you an honest opinion.

- **Was it because of the fit with the institution?**
  Different institutions have different corporate visions and values. For instance, some institutions have set their sights on developing academic medicine, in which case they may favour academically-driven applicants. Other institutions may favour the do-ers over thinkers. Think about how well you align with the institution's vision. If not, is there something that you can change/improve to fit better? If not, you might want to consider trying your luck in another institution in your next MOPEX.

- **Was it to do with interview performance?**
  Check with your colleagues/successful applicants as to how they answered the questions. After each interview, my colleagues and I used to debrief and discuss our answers. This exercise gives you an idea of how else you could improve your answers, whether it is a matter of answering style or distinct argument points/ideas. Given that some of the interview questions can be recycled, this can be really useful for your next round of interviews.

- **Just exactly what was it???**
  It is worth sitting down and getting someone to critically appraise your clinical performance and CV as an evaluation of your chance of success in the application. Truth can be difficult to stomach at times. However, this is a far more efficacious method of identifying gaps, rather than figuring it out by yourself in the dark. Get the person to point out what is lacking in your repertoire and how you could improve on it.

  If you could get one of the consultants on the selection panel to do this for you, it would be great. If not, current registrars/residents can be very helpful too. For one, these are the people who have gone through the selection process recently and thus have a good understanding of the entry requirements. In addition, these groups of people also have a good idea of the department's preference.

  You will find it insightful and really, it will save you the pain of heading in the wrong direction in your next application.

These are painful exercises to go through, but will afford you valuable insight into aspects that you might not have been aware of. It will help you revise your strategies and improve your chances next time round.

2) Reorganise

After an unsuccessful match, one usually has to wait another 4–6 months (match results are released in March/April; next application is in August/September) before the next application.

This doesn't mean holidaying your way till the next application. Until the next application, it is important to fully utilise the time to reorganise your strategies and keep working on the items (clinical rotation/research/poster/presentation/organising an event for the department) that can help increase your chance of success in the next round.

You should try to ensure your next MOPEX is still in the same specialty (assuming that you are still interested in the same specialty). Avoid unwinding too much. Make sure your clinical performance in your day to day work is consistent, if not better. Demonstrate ongoing enthusiasm and interest in the speciality; do adequate preparation before meetings/journal clubs; and study consistently around relevant clinical topics. In addition, it would be helpful to have on-going research projects with the department, and to get involved in presentations or other opportunities to help you stand out.

3) Research

In the US or UK, many doctors who are unmatched take a full year out to do research/MD/PhD. In the US and UK, having an MD or PhD under your belt is looked upon very favourably and increases the applicant's chance in the subsequent match exercise.

While this is a viable option, I am not convinced that it is the best in the local setting. This is of course unless you are research-oriented or have the inclination for a career as a clinician-scientist. It is true that you will be able to carve out a niche for yourself as a research-oriented candidate.

However, given the younger ages of Residency applicants nowadays, (personally) I see more benefit in seeing more breadth in the clinical setting and accumulating more clinical experience. I feel that rather than spending time out of the clinical setting and doing research, being in a clinical rotation, learning how to manage patients and sharpening your clinical acumen prepares you better for Residency training. Regardless of whether the posting is relevant to your specialty of choice, it will give you extra skills that can come in useful. And it shows. In addition, it can broaden your network of friends and contacts whom you will encounter and depend on in your future clinical practice.

Furthermore, research can be done concurrently during a clinical rotation. Better yet, the research that you do within the clinical rotation itself links you to the department. It shows your commitment/contribution to the department and allows your supervisor/department to see your work ethic.

Being in the department allows you time to build rapport with the doctors and staff in the department and gives the department more time to know you.

As an alternative to doing research, others in the US or UK take a year out to teach anatomy/physiology or become facilitators in medical school. Again, this is something that is more common in the US/UK setting compared to ours.

4) Reconsider

There are times where you might want to ask yourself if it is worth persevering. This is a thought that usually surfaces after a few unsuccessful matches, or in face of other considerations such as exhaustion, increasing seniority and conflict in work-life commitments.

To decide on whether to discontinue your pursuit of a specialty or even medicine is something that you should have thorough consideration of before jumping the gun. First, it is worth going through steps 1–3 above.

- **Review** — and see if there is anything else you can change/value-add to your next application. At this stage, you probably want to make sure that whatever change or value that you can add is impactful enough. To get a gauge, you could also speak to the selectors/training programme directors who can give you a realistic gauge of your chance.

- **Reorganise** — and check that you have done everything you could to maximise your chances. Reorganise your thoughts, have a think through your strengths and weaknesses, Figure out where you fit better, aim for what you are good at, work towards it. So, if you are the fish, sign up for the swimming competition rather than the tree-climbing contest.

- **Research/rest of it** — is it worth taking a year out to do something else? It doesn't always have to be research, and can be some other job like teaching anatomy, or any other work that interests you (but still taking the reality of income generation into account). Sometimes taking a year out doing something else may give you a fresh perspective, new orientation and purpose.

In addition, before discontinuing your pursuit of a specialty, it is worth knowing the alternatives.

- Are there other specialties with similar traits that you can or are willing to consider?

- Is being a non-specialist in the institution an option? E.g. Resident physician or service registrar.

- Are there any other specialties which you realistically stand a better chance of entering?

- Is going into private healthcare an option?

- Is quitting medicine an option? Other health-related jobs include: healthcare administration/management jobs, public health jobs, health consulting, healthcare research, and pharmaceutical work.

It is worth weighing the pros and cons of each option, thinking through how they fit with your interest and your life plans. Think it through really hard before making any decisions. If it helps, talk it through with your partner/family/friends. They might be able to give you some opinions and put things into perspective for you.

As per Donald Trump (not the best role model, but this is nevertheless a good quote): "Part of being a winner is knowing when enough is enough. Sometimes you have to give up the fight and walk away, and move on to something that is more productive."

In Summary

Don't be disheartened. Cliché as it sounds. Thomas Edison's teacher told him he was "too stupid to learn anything." Beethoven's teacher called him "hopeless as a composer." Just because you stumble in this part of your journey does not mean that you can't do better later. Chin up whilst being realistic.

Lastly, I will leave you with this quote:

"Successful people don't fear failure, but understand it is necessary to learn and grow from." — Robert Kiyosaki.

Index